Chicago's Unique Miniature Operas:

Chicago Puppet Opera
Kungsholm Miniature Grand Opera
Opera in Focus

by

Luman Coad

cp

Library and Archives Canada Cataloguing in Publication Data

Title: Chicago's miniature grand operas : Chicago Miniature Opera, Kungsholm Miniature Grand Opera,

 Opera in Focus / Luman Coad.

Names: Coad, Luman, author.

Identifiers: Canadiana 2019011276X | ISBN 9780921845508 (softcover) | 978-0-921845-57-7 (hardcover)

Subjects: LCSH: Puppet theater—United States—History. | LCSH: Puppet making—United States—History.

 | LCSH: Opera—Illinois—Chicago.

Classification: LCC PN1978 U6 C65 2019 | DDC 791.5/30977311—dc23

ISBN: 978-0-921845-57-7

Charlemagne Press
Garden Bay, BC
V0N 1S1 Canada
www.charlemagnepress.com

Thank You

My deepest gratitude to the many people who enthusiastically encouraged, aided, and advised in the creation of this study. In alphabetical order, thank you:

Steve Abrams, *Puppetry Journal*, Philadelphia, PA

Britta Keller Arendt, Chicago History Museum, Chicago, IL

John Bell, Ballard Institute and Museum of Puppetry, University of Connecticut, Storrs, CT

Ronnie Burkett, Toronto, ON

Dmitri Carter, Northwest Puppet Center, Seattle, WA

Mary Decker, San Diego, CA

Rose Grossinger, Lincolnwood IL

David Herzog, Chicago, IL

Gary Jones, Los Angeles, CA

Yanique Leonard, Center for Puppetry Arts, Atlanta, GA

Katie Levi, Chicago History Museum, Chicago, IL

Jill Nash Malool, Center for Puppetry Arts, Atlanta, GA

Fred and Marilyn Putz, Chicago, IL

Pix Smith, Dallas, TX

Justin Snyder, Opera in Focus, Rolling Hills, IL

Shannon Tauschman, Lawry's The Prime Rib, Chicago, IL

Keith Ulrich, Swedish American Museum, Chicago, IL

Harold Washington Library Center, Chicago, IL

Emily Wicks, Ballard Institute and Museum of Puppetry, University of Connecticut, Storrs, CT

Photo Credits

Contents

Yvonne Chauveau, setting up for *Madame Butterfly*,
was one of Chramer's assistants when the
Kungsholm Miniature Grand Opera opened in 1941.

Introduction

AS THE HOUSE LIGHTS fade, the audience settles into quiet expectation. The tuxedo attired conductor appears in the orchestra pit and bows gallantly to the audience's applause. He turns to his orchestra, lifts his baton, and the overture begins. The red and gold curtain rises to reveal a stunning set. Elegantly costumed players enter and the story begins to unfold. A typical beginning of an opera performance.

But wait. Something is very odd.

These performers are not much larger than Barbie dolls. Watching them is akin to sitting in the last row of the upper balcony of a very large opera house.

For more than eighty years Chicago has been home to a unique form of theatre – miniature grand opera. The genre began in a residential basement when a boy began re-enacting opera scenes with small stationary figures to the music played on 78 rpm records. Within a few years the miniature opera, with articulated figures, was performing to full houses at the 1939 New York World's Fair. It became the after-dinner entertainment at one of Chicago's most elegant restaurants where it entranced even the very opera stars heard on the recordings during the performances. And it survives today in a bijou basement theatre in a Chicago suburb.

This book follows the origins of the diminutive opera, its emergence into Chicago's social scene, and its present day near-obscurity. The story of the three separate opera companies and their entrepreneurs has as many twists and turns as any opera plot.

And it is unique to Chicago.

1 – Ernest and Esther Wolff
Chicago Miniature Opera Theater

C HICAGO'S EIGHT DECADES of miniature grand opera began with the obsession of a twelve year old lad.

In 1925, Mrs. Esther T. Wolff[1] took her son Ernest[2] to a performance of *"Carmen"* at the Chicago Auditorium. "At that moment," he later recounted, "I became an opera addict for life. It was not just the music, it was the combination of spectacle, lighting, singing, costumes, color, motion, and grandeur."[3]

Ernest began to collect opera records and whenever possible, he would attend live performances then sketch the scenery and craft miniature cardboard settings on a stage he had devised from an orange crate. This stage gave way to an improved model using Christmas tree lights for the footlights and old flashlights modified into spotlights.

A similar form of theater, known as "toy theater," "miniature theater," "paper theater", or "juvenile theater", had originated during the early 1800's in Europe. Heavy paper pages, printed with a theater proscenium, were available either coloured or uncoloured to allow the purchaser to paint an individualized theater. The sheets would then be mounted on heavier card stock, the pieces cut out and clipped to a simple wooden frame work. Separate kits of different plays, complete with scenery, furniture, props and actors, were also available. The flat figures of the actors would be mounted to

Model Theater
c. 1870[4]

a wooden or metal base to keep them standing upright and a stiff wire, attached to the base was operated from the side of the stage to move the figures about the setting.[5]

Ernest, however, decided to populate his model settings with dimensional figures rather than flat cardboard cut-outs. He modeled clay figures in operatic poses and his mother, a trained couturiere, researched costumes from the New York Metropolitan Opera, the Paris Opera, the La Scala in Milan, and the Chicago Civic Opera. She then sewed miniature duplicates for the clay figures.

Desiring to bring some of the thrill of grand opera to his friends and to other music lovers who couldn't afford to attend live operas, Ernest arranged an evening "show" in the family basement consisting of tableaus of six opera arias. The curtain would rise on the scene with the characters already in place, the music would play from a Victrola, and at the end of the aria the curtain would close. The figures never moved and the audiences began asking, "Can't you give your figures some action so they appear alive?"[6]

Mrs. Wolff found some realistic adult German dolls with porcelain heads on sawdust stuffed cloth bodies and loose, dangling arms and legs. Although they were only available as male and female figures, characters could be individualized by repainting the face, adding a wig, wrapping extra padding around the body to alter the figure's silhouette, and of course, by the costume.

But how to animate the figures? Marionettes were rejected because their strings would tangle in the overhead lights and the puppets would not be able to pass through doorways. The solution was to operate the figures from beneath the stage floor. The inspiration may have been the Ukrainian *vertep*, a seasonal folk puppet show which Mrs. Wolff could have seen in Czechoslovakia when she was young.

The *vertep* puppet stage is a shallow box structure with two, but sometimes three, levels. The floor of each level has a crosswise slot so the simple puppets on sticks or wires can be moved across the stage without the puppeteer's hands intruding into the scene.

Mrs. Wolff stitched a length of coat hanger wire to the back of each doll which projected down through slots in the stage floor. By wiggling the wire, the figure on stage could be moved to the music.

As word spread, audiences quickly outgrew the limited cellar space. Ernest began to charge a small admission fee and used the income to finance further refinements – a quality electric phonograph, better lighting, and such.

As the productions grew more elaborate, Ernest designed and built a larger, portable stage complete with a fly gallery to lift backdrops out of sight above the proscenium. Parallel slots ran across the stage and a central front-to-back slot

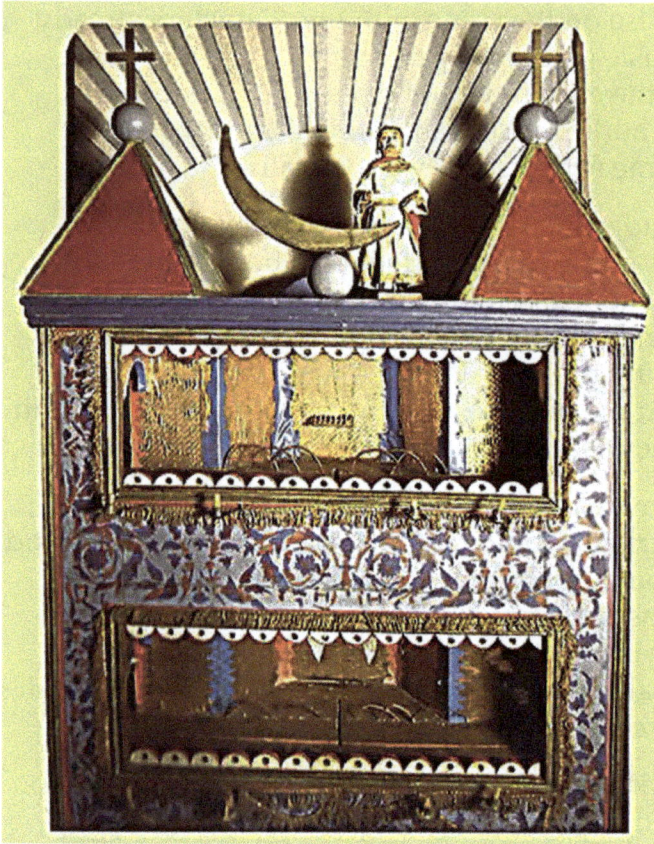

Ukrainian *Vertep* Theater[7]

enabled the puppets to move upstage or down.[8] The entire construction, weighing some 3,000 pounds, could be dismantled for transport in about thirty minutes.[9]

Eventually five people, including Mrs. Wolff, operated the puppets in the four foot space beneath the stage floor. Each puppeteer sat on a low rolling stool and peered up through the narrow slots to observe their puppet's actions. The company was expanded to include an electrician who controlled the increasingly complicated stage lighting, a sound technician who ensured the music flowed seamlessly from one 78 record to the next, and a business manager. Ernest, as the director and producer, rarely operated the puppets.[10]

Stick puppets created by the Wolffs from commercial German dolls.

"Carmen," "Aida," "Faust," and *"Pagliacci"* were some of the first operas to be produced in miniature and by 1935, *"La Boheme," "Die Valküre,"* and *"Salome"* had joined the repertoire. On November 10, 1936, the newly named Chicago Miniature Opera Theater opened to a small audience with a complete performance of *"Aida"* and was soon booked to entertain at ladies clubs, musical societies, lodges, social groups, and schools in the Chicago area.[11]

Word of the miniature opera spread beyond Chicago and Ernest's company was recruited to perform for six months in the Gas Industries of America pavilion at the 1939 New York World's Fair. Sponsored by the Victor Record Company, professional quality sound equipment was acquired while the stage and puppets were enlarged. The German dolls were no longer available so Mrs. Wolff and Fred Stauffer, a family friend, devised a 13" tall puppet – described in Appendix 1.

The Chicago Miniature Opera Theater was renamed the American Puppet Opera Company then just before the premiere, the name was changed to the Victor Puppet Opera. [12]

A young music lover enjoying Ernest Wolff's presentation of "Rigoletto." Note the puppet orchestra

BOY'S HOBBY CREATES

Puppet Opera

Wolff shows Helen Jepson, noted opera star, a puppet wearing a reproduction of one of Miss Jepson's own costumes

THIRTEEN years ago, in a Chicago basement, a twelve-year-old schoolboy, Ernest Wolff, began experimenting with puppets synchronized with opera recordings. His stage was an old apple crate, draped with cloth from his mother's sewing box; his illumination, a string of lights from the Christmas tree; his puppets, ordinary dolls.

Until that time, young Ernest had been just a typical

POPULAR SCIENCE

- 6 -

American boy, with a boy's disdain for anything that smacked of "high art." However, a visit to an opera in Europe gave him a strange jolt. The presentation was "Carmen." He was thrilled not only with the music, but with the elaborate lighting and staging. When he got back to Chicago he went to every performance of "Carmen" he could manage to see, getting in some way when he couldn't raise the money to pay.

Opera soon began to saturate his living. In his spare time he studied the lives of composers and artists, hummed tunes, made sketches of scenery and costumes he had seen at the Chicago Civic Opera. It was his ambition to devise a means to bring some of the thrill of grand opera to his friends, and to other music lovers who could not afford to attend a real performance by living singers.

The apple-box stage, with its crude scenery, puppets, and lighting, was the beginning. At first, just a few friends were invited to witness the performances. Soon, however, the news spread, and neighbors and friends were flocking down into his basement "opera house" in such numbers that he had to charge a small admission fee to hold back the crowds!

With these fees, and every other cent he could save, Ernest Wolff kept building and rebuilding his miniature operas, aiming each time to come nearer the smooth perfection of a real opera. Finally outgrowing his basement auditorium, he built a portable outfit and gave performances before women's clubs and music societies throughout Chicago. Today, the twenty-five-year-old impresario is showing his miniature operas before music lovers in cities from New York to San Francisco, with no let-up in sight for future engagements.

Designed entirely by Wolff, and built largely by him and his company of assistants, the present opera equipment is a triumph of miniature stagecraft. Believing that the frivolousness of the average puppet show is out of place in a serious opera, he has striven for realism throughout.

The cast consists of nearly 200 thirteen-inch puppet opera stars, with a wardrobe of 300 hand-sewn miniature costumes, each authentic in every detail. To produce this huge cast, Wolff first modeled two standard heads in clay—one of a man, and the other a woman. From these models, wooden heads were

By
ARTHUR A. STUART

•

Sliding about on "dollies" under the floor of the miniature stage, puppeteers operate the tiny figures by means of rods and wires. The dolls move along slots in the floor

turned out wholesale on a carving machine. The wooden heads were then given individual character by appropriate painting and wigs. Bodies were made for the puppets by means of wire and padding.

To permit the amazing scenic and lighting effects of a real opera production, ordinary marionettes worked by strings were out of the question. Stringed puppets could not go through gates and doorways; an overhead puppeteers' loft would interfere with lights and scenery. A mechanism therefore had to be devised whereby the puppets could be operated realistically from beneath the stage. The problem was finally solved by having stiff wires, extending down through the body, work the arms and head, the puppets

A puppeteer displays the mechanism of one of the "characters." At the right are some of the 300 costumes designed and made by Wolff's mother. Many of them were patterned after the costumes used in famous European and American opera companies. The picture at top of page shows how it looks to an audience

- 8 -

Miniature period furniture being built and upholstered for "La Traviata." Most of the tiny stage "props" were made by hand

Wolff at work on artificial greenery to decorate a setting. Every piece of equipment is realistic. In the background are puppet heads

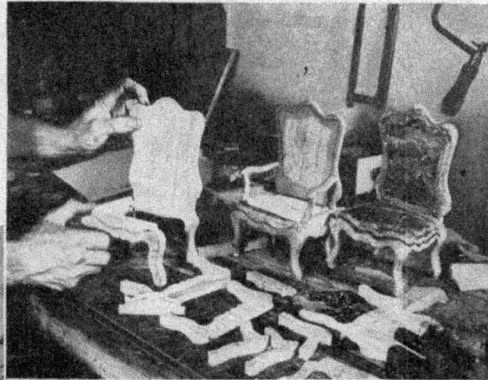

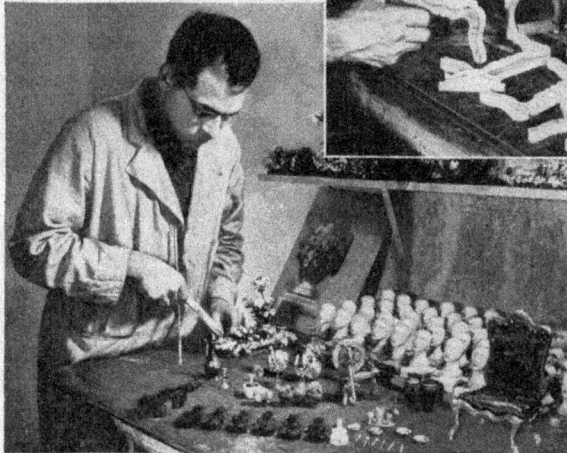

Below, the make-up artist at work. "Blank" heads of wood are given individual characteristics through wigs and painted facial features

moving about along paths formed by a series of slots cut in the stage.

The stage properties, most of which were made by hand, include three complete suits of period furniture, spinning wheels, tables, chairs, fireplaces, vases, candlesticks, silverware, jewel boxes, couches, lanterns, chandeliers, donkey carts, and many other pieces.

A chandelier used in "La Traviata" was constructed from 3,000 crystals, and another for "Rigoletto" was made of brass and consists of sixty candelabra. In "Carmen," the soldiers' helmets are made of brass and fashioned entirely by hand. The felt hats in "Faust" were blocked on specially carved miniature wood hat blocks.

In this opera, "Faust," occur a few amazing tricks of puppetry. Mephistopheles, the devil, is made to appear and disappear out of sudden gusts of thin white smoke. Within sight of the audience, the old, white-bearded Faust is transformed suddenly into the young, dashing, beardless suitor of the beautiful Marguerite. The substitution is really adept sleight-of-hand, aided by a

trapdoor in the stage, while the gusts of "white vapors" are puffs of tobacco smoke, blown up through a slot in the stage by one of the puppeteers!

All the settings used in the puppet operas are adaptations of scenery used by the La Scala Opera of Milan, Italy, the Metropolitan Opera of New York, and the Chicago Civic Opera Company. To add to the realism, a twenty-one-piece puppet orchestra begins tuning up its fiddles before each act. A frowzy-haired puppet conductor, known intimately as "Toscanini," then appears, takes a bow, and proceeds to lead his orchestra in a beautiful overture.

This realism extends to every piece of

Behind the scenes of the puppet opera. On the left is the switchboard that controls the elaborate lighting effects, on the right the phonograph turntables. Above, a scene from "Faust," as seen from the wings

mantled and made ready for shipment by truck in about half an hour.

Holding for himself the title of producer and director, Ernest Wolff now has eight assistants, including five puppeteers, an electrician, a sound man, and a business manager. Like himself, all his puppet operators are linguists and musicians. They learn every opera by heart, and try to express each nuance of word and musical movement through the motions of the tiny actors. Each opera requires a month of difficult rehearsing, during which Ernest sits out front, suggesting movements of puppets' heads, hands, and legs, synchronized with the recorded music, while the puppeteers beneath the stage take notes.

Even the sound man, who shifts the phonograph records and watches over the reproducing equipment, is a musician, and works from a musical score. Sometimes well-known American operatic stars, such as Lily Pons, Helen Jepson, or Lawrence Tibbett, are cut into an opera to sing a famous aria. In each case, the sound man knows to a breath where the aria begins and ends on a record. Often the realism is so great, and the music so moving, that audiences have been known to rise after an aria, shouting "Bravo! Bravo!" and refusing to quiet down until the puppet gave an encore!

back-stage equipment. Scenery consists of regulation "flats," "drops," and "borders," with a blue cyclorama encircling the back of the stage. Flats are fastened to the forty-eight square feet of stage space with miniature stage braces. When scenes are shifted, drops that must be gotten out of the way are hoisted into a regular fly loft overhead. Specially built miniature spotlights and floodlights are all under the control of an elaborate switchboard.

The stage was constructed for extreme mobility, without a single nail or screw. By removing a few hooks, nuts, and wedges, the entire 3,000-pound structure can be dis-

In the course of his cross-country tour, combined with special engagements of longer duration, Wolff has exhibited his puppet operas to more than a quarter of a million people. Musicians and educators have acclaimed his work for its value in spreading the appreciation of operatic music. And, he has brought a new experience into the lives of thousands who would never have set foot inside a great opera house.

88

A larger stage, measuring six feet wide and eight feet deep was built. Seven new productions were created with the new, larger puppets - *"Faust," "Hansel and Gretel," "I Pagliacci," "La Traviata," "Carmen," "Rigoletto,"* and *"Aida."* The latter production featured seventy-five soldiers, slaves, camels, and elephants in the second act's Triumphal March. The orchestra now had twenty-one puppet musicians plus the conductor and the crew of manipulators was increased to seven.[13]

The six month contract required one opera to be performed for an entire week with four half-hour performances each afternoon and the full-length opera in the evening.[14] About 1,800 people saw the Victor Puppet Opera each day at the World's Fair.[15]

When the engagement ended, the Victor Puppet Opera began touring in the Midwest – performing primarily in audtoriums of larger department stores, in school assembly rooms, and occasionally in a theater.[16]

As the U.S. prepared to enter World War Two, Ernest enlisted in the Navy and a farewell tour of the Victor Puppet Opera was arranged. The final performances would be at DePaul University's Kimball Hall in Chicago.

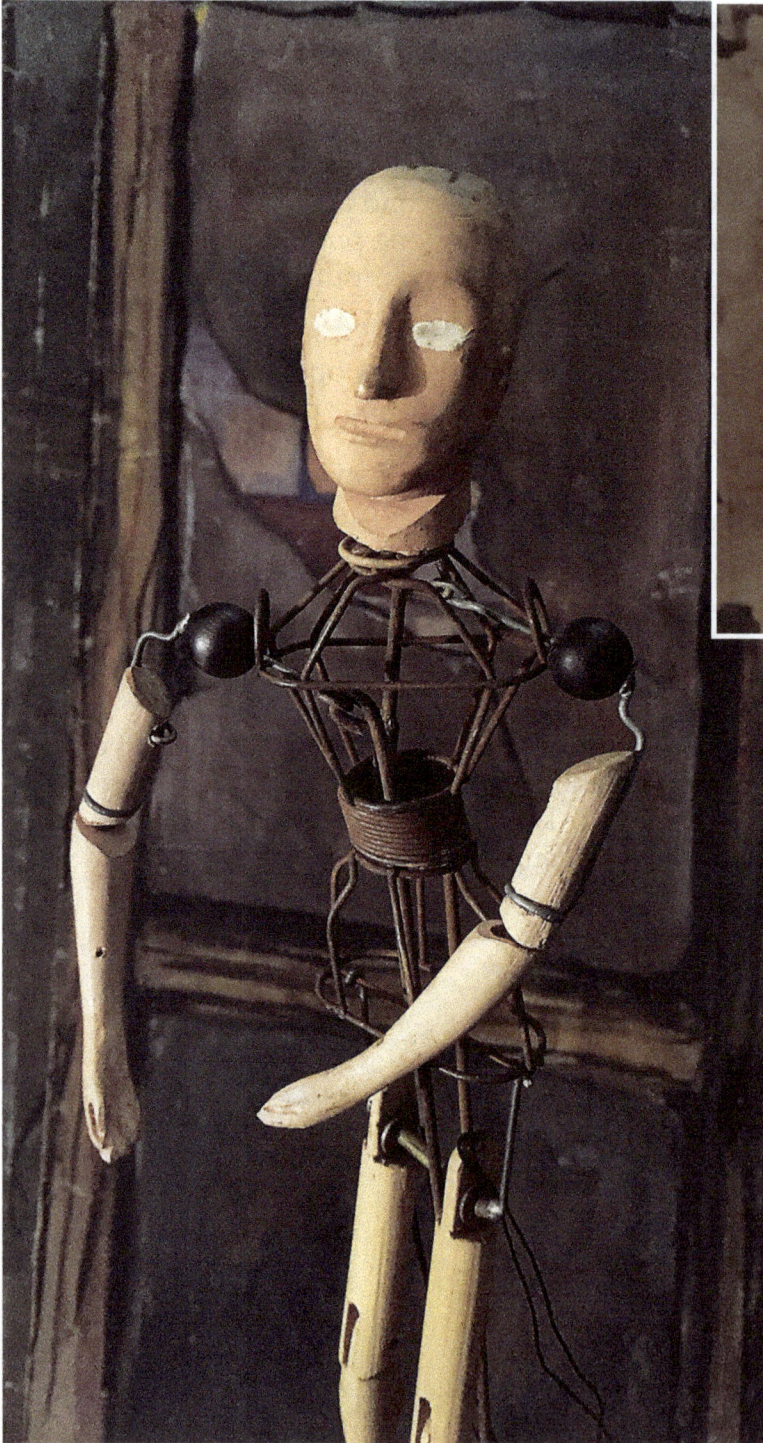

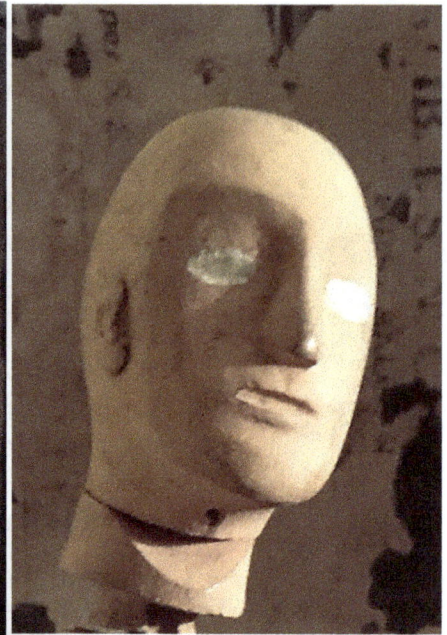

Wire cage body
with basic
male head.

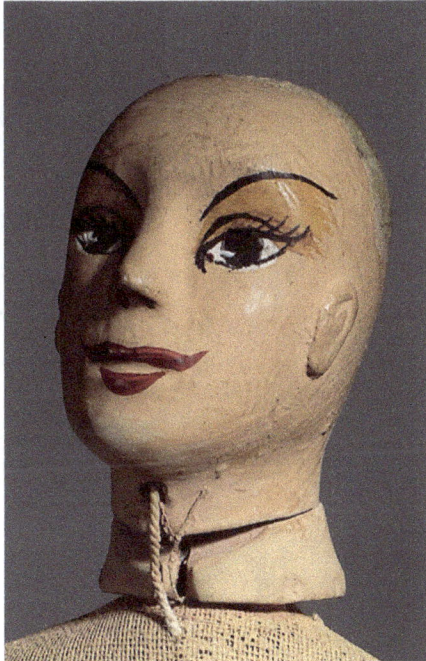

Wire cage body
with silhouette
padding and basic
female head.

Chicago History Museum
iCHI176221

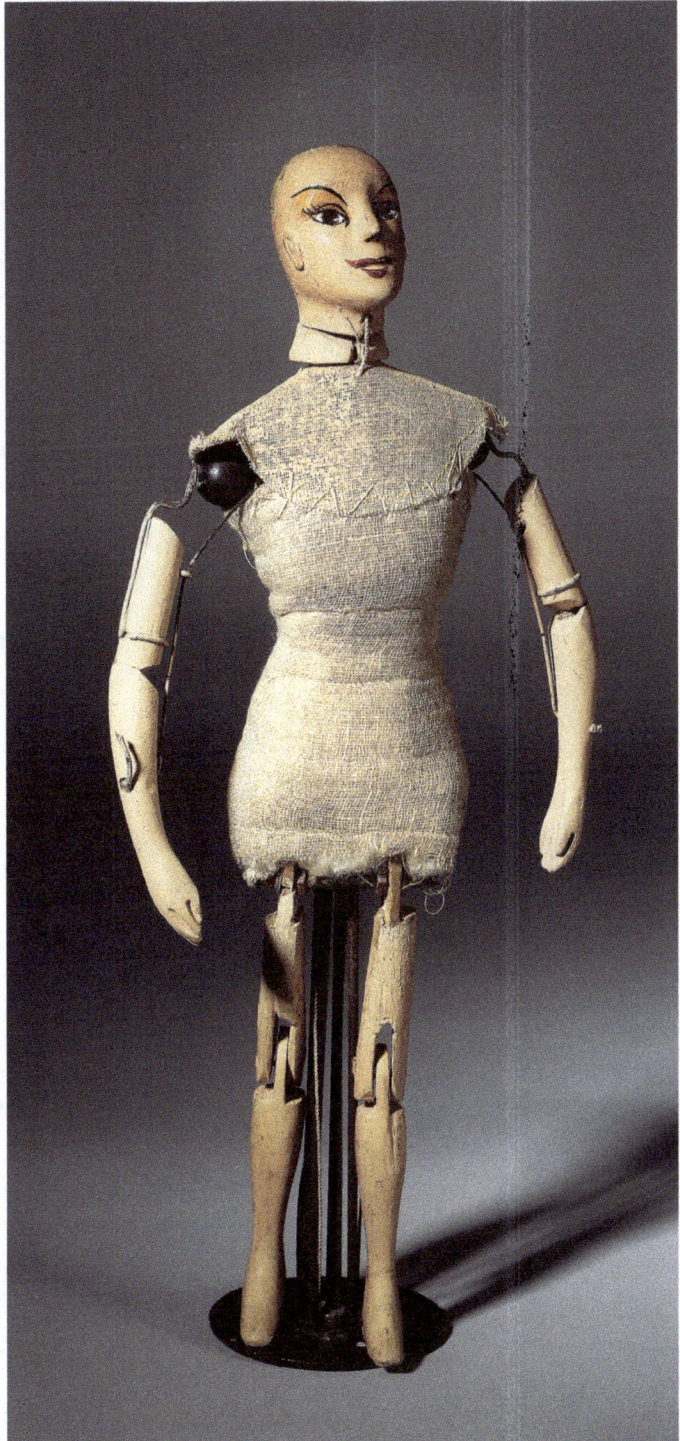

Violetta

"La Traviata"

Chicago History Museum
ICHI: 176223

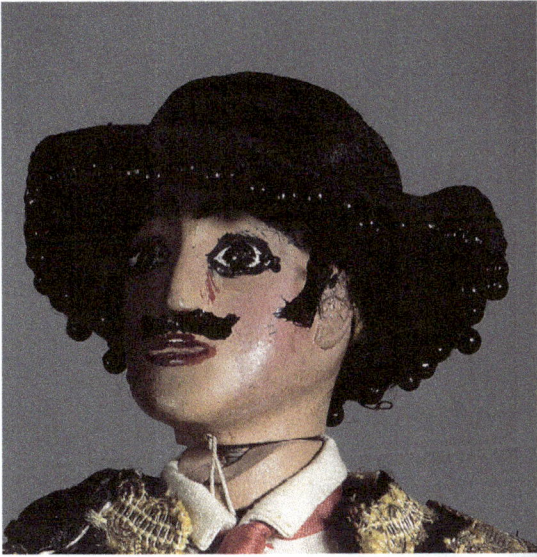

Escamillo

"Carmen"

Chicago History
Museum

ICHI: 176218

Brünnhilde

"Die Walküre"

Chicago History
Museum

ICHI: 176219

Canio

"I Pagliacci"

Chicago History
Museum

ICHI: 176220

Floria

"Tosca"

Chicago History
Museum
ICHI: 176222

Cho-Cho-San

"Madama Butterfly"

Chicago History
Museum

ICHI: 176217

[1] Esther Theresa Wolff was born 1883 in Austria to parents from Czechoslovakia. She died in 1972. www.ancestry.com

[2] Ernest Wolff was born in 1913 died in 1972. www.ancestry.com

[3] *Chicago Guide*, n.d., n.p.

[4] Courtesy: Baldwin, Peter, *Toy Theatres of the World*, Zwemmer, London, 1992.

[5] https://en.wikipedia.org/wiki/

[6] *Chicago Guide*, n.d., n.p.

[7] Courtesy: UNIMA-Ukraine.

[8] The term 'upstage' means towards the back of the stage while "downstage" means towards the audience. The terms originated when stage floors were sloped towards the audience.

[9] Stuart, Arthur, "Boy's Hobby Creates Puppet Opera," *Popular Science*, April, 1940, p. 84-88.

[10] McPharlin, Paul, *Puppet Theater in America: A History, 1524 to 1948 with a Supplement, Puppets in America since 1948* by Marjorie Batchelder McPharlin. Plays Inc, Boston, 1969. p. 481.

[11] Bauman, Thomas, "Opera", *Encyclopedia of Chicago*. (www.encyclopedia.chicagohistory.org/pages/3597.html)

[12] Letter from Irwin A. Shame to Ernest Wolff, February 15, 1947.

[13] "Gas Industries Exhibit will present Puppet Opera at Fair" *A.G.S.A.E.M. Bulletin*, March 1939. p. 7.

[14] *Chicago Guide*, Vol. 20, No. 7, July, 1971, p. 18.

[15] *Victor Record Review*, Vol. 2, No. 2, June, 1939. n.p.

[16] Undated newspaper ads in Esther Wolff's scrapbook.

2 – Fredrik A. Chramer
Kungsholm Miniature Grand Opera

WHEN FREDRIK A. CHRAMER[1] was nine years old, his grandfather made a toy theater and Fredrik's life-long fascination with opera began. He came to the U.S. from Denmark in 1908 at the age 18 but there are no records of him during the next three decades. He obviously learned the restaurant business – possibly becoming a maître d' or manager at an upper scale restaurant. By 1937 he had the money or financial backing to lease the Leander Hamilton McCormick mansion, extensively renovate it, and open the elegant Kungsholm Scandinavian Restaurant.

The Leander Hamilton McCormick mansion was a four storey, 25 room Italianate style building at the corner of Rush and Ontario Streets – a section of the Near North neighbourhood called "McCormickville" because a number of McCormick family homes were in the area.[2]

Leander Hamilton McCormick[3] was a nephew of Cyrus H. McCormick who had patented a horse-drawn farm reaping machine and founded the McCormick Harvesting Machine Company which later became part of International Harvester Company.

Leander graduated from Amherst College in 1881. He studied law at Columbia University then, for a while, took up architecture. On February 15, 1887[4], he married Constance Plummer[5] of Canterbury, England, and the couple commissioned the internationally famous architect, Stanford White, to design their residence in Chicago. The mansion cost $125,000 (about $3.5 million today[6]). The bricks were imported from Belgium – each wrapped in straw like a bottle of fine wine. The interior featured exquisitely carved oak and Honduras mahogany woodwork. The ballroom on the fourth floor could accommodate 400 guests. Numerous social functions and elegant dinners were hosted by the couple with the guest list including such dignitaries as the Duke of Kent and the Prince of Wales.[7]

L.H. McCormick
Mansion
circa 1935

In the very early 20th Century, the mansion was leased to a succession of prominent families when the McCormicks moved to London and began collecting paintings, sculptures, old armor, and objets d'art.[8] At the beginning of the First World War, they returned to Chicago with their impressive collections and resumed hosting social gatherings at the mansion.

Leander is credited with more than a hundred inventions and a number of patents[9]. He also became a published authority on characterology – a system for "assessing an individual's character through a scientific, objective examination of their physical appearance."[10]

When he died in 1934, Constance rented the mansion and moved to a hotel. Fredrik Chramer leased the building in 1937, renovated the interior in blue and gold Swedish Modern style, and opened the Kungsholm Scandinavian Restaurant. The renovations cost $63,000 (over $1 million today[11]). Shortly before her death, Mrs. McCormick dined at the Kungsholm and said to Chramer, "My, if I had known it could be redecorated in such grand style, I would have hesitated about renting it to you."[12]

Kungsholm's piano-shaped smörgåsbord table.

The Kungsholm Scandinavian Restaurant was known for its elaborate and colourful smörgåsbord of cold and hot Scandinavian foods arranged buffet-style on a large, piano-shaped table. The meal began by selecting from the cold dishes.

Pickled herring, prepared in several different ways, was always offered. For the next course, a fresh plate was filled with warm delicacies from the table – meat balls, Swedish beans, etc. Then came a soup followed by a choice of entrée. The dinner concluded with a dessert followed by coffee and perhaps, brandy or punch.[13]

Chramer turned the fourth floor ballroom into a private movie theater where his friends and select restaurant patrons were invited to watch his color movies as well as sports, educational, travel, and war films.[14]

In October, 1941 when the Wolffs' Victor Puppet Opera Company farewell tour concluded with a week of shows at Kimball Hall in Chicago, Chramer attended one of the performances and wanted to buy the miniature opera to install in the fourth floor theater at the Kungsholm Restaurant. The Wolffs agreed to help Chramer get started. Mrs. Wolff would operate the theatre using the Wolffs' company of puppeteers and technicians. That way their company would not be disbanded while Ernest was in the military.[15]

Ernest prepared designs and sketches for the stage plus scenery for *"Triviata," "Rigoletto," "Madame Butterfly," "Tosca,"* and *"Il Trovatore."* The Wolffs loaned their puppets until Chramer could have a new set created.

Because Ernest was polylingual[16], he served two years at the Naval Attaché's office at the consulate in Curaçao then at the American embassy in Lisbon for two and a half years – apparently working as an undercover agent.[17]

When the Kungsholm Miniature Grand Opera opened in 1941, Chramer claimed full credit for the concept of performing grand opera with puppets.[18] The Wolffs were not even mentioned. Mrs. Wolff objected but Chramer said the show was his property and he could say and do as he wished. When Mrs. Wolff pointed out the puppets were not Chramer's property, Chramer promised to revise the new printed

Kungsholm's proscenium was inspired by the Chicago Civic Opera's proscenium.

programs. But this didn't happen and when others had been trained to perform Mrs. Wolff's duties, she was dismissed.[19]

In Curaçao, Ernest happened to see a newsreel story of the Kungsholm Miniature Grand Opera. In the film, Chramer again claimed the entire enterprise was his creation.[20]

Mrs. Wolff filed a patent application for the unique rod puppet she and Fred Stauffer had created. The application included the adjustable slotted stage floor Ernest had devised.[21] The Kungsholm performances continued without pause.

In a 1945 interview Chramer said Lauritz Melchior and Kirsten Flagstad were his dinner guests after they had sung *Tristan and Isolde* at the Chicago Civic Opera House. To compliment them, he had a puppet Tristan and a puppet Isolde enact a recording of their love duet on the stage of the restaurant's fourth floor movie theater. He said the guests were so charmed, he decided to present puppet grand opera every night.[22] But the decision to present the after-dinner

STRINGLESS PUPPETS PUT ON GRAND OPERA

GRAND opera, with stringless puppets instead of real singers strutting about a miniature stage, is the culmination of a lifelong hobby of Fredrik Chramer, Chicago restaurant owner. The 13-inch puppets, the scenery, the theater with 95 fixed seats, the stage and the production reflect many years of painstaking work and research. Unlike marionettes controlled from above by strings, these tiny figures, clad in costumes copied from those worn by Metropolitan and LaScala artists, respond to the deft manipulation of wires passing downward through slots in the stage floor that form "tracks" for the cast. Four girls, maneuvering the puppets from beneath the stage, wear headphones to keep in touch with Mr. Chramer, who directs each presentation. Orchestral music and the voices of many famous artists come from disk recordings. Remarkable for beauty and com-

Typical of other puppets, Flora of La Traviata, above, is controlled by looped wires and rods. A disk at the feet enables puppet to stand erect

Below, left, a corner in the workshop where scenery and properties are built by expert workmen. Right, looking through stage wings. Rows of overhead lights may be raised and lowered. More than 1,000 lights are used, some being operated from backstage, others from the control room

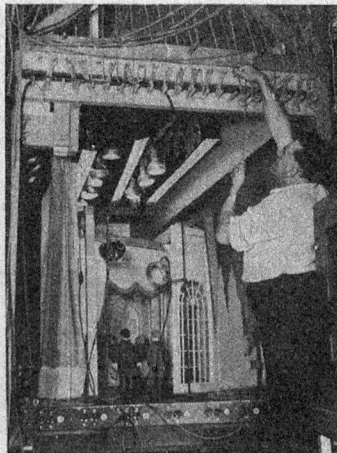

14 POPULAR MECHANICS

Girls beneath stage see that puppets do not miss
cues and give them action appropriate to music

pleteness, the scenery and properties
are constructed in Mr. Chramer's own
workshop. Since an operatic performance calls for little more than slight
gestures, the puppets' actions are limited to simple arm, leg and head movements, yet they can kneel, sit, shake
hands, embrace and even carry small
articles. For his repertoire of 14 operas,
Mr. Chramer uses about 300 puppets,
48 being the largest number for any
single performance.

In control room Mr. Chramer runs disks, operates most
of stage lights by bank of switches. Below, scene from
La Traviata; note tiny candelabra, puppet orchestra with
leader "Tosci." Stage is 12 feet wide, eight feet high

entertainment had already been made prior to that evening – how else would Chramer have been able to re-create the duet with puppets?

Two years after its premier, the Kungsholm Miniature Grand Opera repertoire had grown to fourteen operas with 300 puppets.

Chramer preferred to hire female puppeteers because he felt they had more natural "sophistication and grace" where-as men have a tendency to be clunky and heavy-handed.[23] Puppeteers operating the figures from beneath the slotted stage floor wore headphones to hear Mr. Chramer's directions from the control booth at the back of the theater.[24] Their work was not limited to manipulating the puppets in eighteen performances each week. In operatic repertory tradition, the production was replaced daily with a different opera.[25] This daily change entailed long hours of shifting scenery, switching casts of puppets, and brush-up rehears-als. Chramer stated the opera cost about $3000.00 per month (nearly $34,000 today[26]) to operate in 1947.

Returning to Chicago after the war, Ernest Wolff launched a lawsuit claiming Fredrik Chramer had stolen his creation.[27] The Wolffs then built a new stage and repertoire of operas and resumed their pre-war touring in the Midwest.[28]

Above: Theater Lobby

Left: Melchoir Dining Room

Below: Viking Lounge

"Aida"
circa 1945

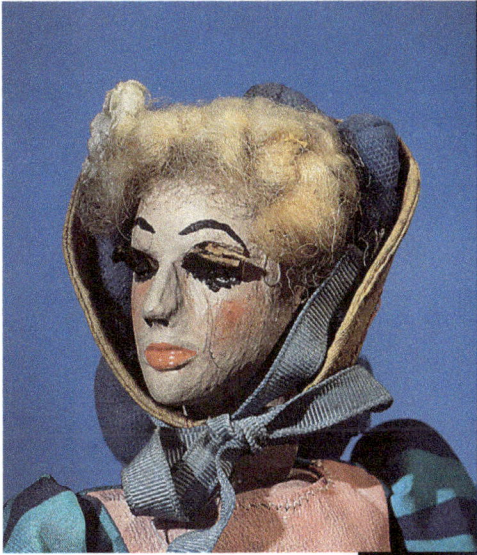

Chorus member

"La Boheme"

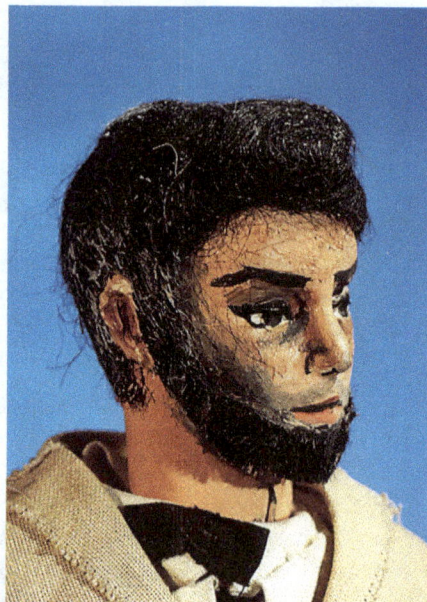

(Unidentified)

Chorus Member

"Carmen"

(Unidentified)

(Unidentified)

Both Pages:

(Unidentified)

Chorus Member

"Camelot"

(Unidentified)

Entrance to Grand Opera Theatre

SOUVENIR PROGRAM

KUNGSHOLM
MINIATURE GRAND OPERA THEATRE
CHICAGO

Grand Opera Theatre

(My first Opera Theatre at age of nine)

This evening you have been invited as my guest, to the Kungsholm Miniature Grand Opera Theater created for the pleasure of my guests and friends who like it and I do hope you will enjoy the performance which I have planned for you as much as I enjoy having you here; therefore I would greatly appreciate my guests refraining from conversation or leaving the auditorium during the performance, as it may disturb the audience.

Fine Operas and good music are my hobbies and have been for many years (in fact I presented my first Puppet Opera to my schoolmates when I was nine years of age); from them I have gained not only limitless pleasures, but relaxation from business as well; consequently my approach in building this Opera Theatre has realized my life long dream and has been a personal one for the joy and satisfaction it gives also an outlet for creative instincts.

This Opera Theatre has been built to bring forth the true picture of the fine Operas which the Victor, as well as the Columbia Recording Companies have so successfully produced from the two great Opera Companies La Scala Milan and L'Opera Paris-France. Guest artists all via recording, such as Lauritz Melchior, Kirsten Flagstad, Tibbet, Crooks, Schorr, Lotte Lehmann, Jepson, Bjoerling, Pons, Thomas, Martinelli, Giannini are heard during some of the performances.

To present my repertoire of twenty-eight operas, which I have in my music library, consisting of forty Victor and Columbia musical masterpiece albums, a total of four hundred twenty records—"840"-sides are reproduced by the latest RCA commercial sound equipment through the new type of Peter Jensen's loud speakers.

A personnel of thirteen people are required to perform the numerous understage and backstage operations including manipulating of the stringless Puppets, operating the electric control board and the sound system, shifting scenery between acts, changing costumes, wigs and make-up. The seven hundred Puppets who sing, dance, love, fight and die in my Opera productions are operated from below the forty-eight square foot stage, by five trained operators, who are music students and know each Opera note for note.

An extensive wardrobe consisting of more than twelve hundred Opera costumes is required, supplemented by hats, wigs, silk stockings, shirts, silk tights, aprons, boots and shoes. Each costume is an exact copy (in miniature) of those worn by Metropolitan and La Scala Opera Artists.

Two hundred forty pieces of scenery and set-pieces, include street scenes, gardens, palace interiors, a bull arena, mountains, forests, a prison, houses, stair-ways, bed-rooms, churches, brick walls, rocks, bridges, etcetera.

The lighting equipment consists of eighty-eight footlights, eighty-eight proscenium lights, twenty-four flood and twenty-four miniature spot lights and twelve hundred border lights.

The chandelier seen in the first act of La Traviata was constructed from genuine Czecho-Slovakian crystal, while the one in the third act is of brass and has forty-two candalabras.

The full size Opera Orchestra of twenty-five Puppets is complete with violins, cellos, bass violins, harp, clarionets, flutes, french horns, bassoons, kettle drums and other orchestral instruments.

The diminutive conductor "Tosci" leads the Puppet musicians in perfect tempo with the music.

Stage properties comprise a fine collection of miniatures and consist of three complete suites of period furniture, spinning wheel, tables, chairs, fire-places, clocks, vases, candlesticks, plates, jewel boxes, couches, lanterns, chandeliers, donkey carts, love seats and many other pieces, most of which are produced in my own work shop.

Permit me at this time to thank you for your valuable patronage at the Kungsholm, and I wish to extend to you and your guests the invitation to be present at a performance in my home Miniature Opera Theatre any evening soon.

Fredrik A. Cramer

KUNGSHOLM MINIATURE OPERA COMPANY

(Created for my guests and friends who like it)

FREDRIK A. CHRAMER
General Director

Presents

I PAGLIACCI

Opera in Two Acts by Ruggiero Leoncavallo

CAST OF CHARACTERS

NEDDA (in the play "Columbine"), a strolling player,
wife of Canio...IVA PACETTI, *Soprano*

CANIO (in the play "Pagliaccio"),   GIOVANNI MARTINELLI, *Tenor*
master of the troupe....................   BENIAMINO GIGLI, *Tenor*

                                                         LAWRENCE TIBBETT, *Baritone*
TONIO (in the play "Taddeo"), the Clown....   MARIO BASIOLA, *Baritone*

PEPPE (in the play "Harlequin")........................GIUSEPPE NESSI, *Tenor*

SILVIO (a villager)....................................LEONE PASSE, *Baritone*

VILLAGERS and PEASANTS

Members of the Chorus and Orchestra of La Scala, Milan

—

The performance conducted by Maestro Franco Ghione

—

The Scene is laid in Calabria, near Montalto, on the Feast of the Virgin di Mezzagosto

Period: Between 1865 and 1870

A Victor Standard Musical Masterpiece
Kungsholm Miniature Opera Conductor "Tosci"
Staged and directed by Fredrik A. Chramer
Stage property built by Mr. Odin Ostness
Stage exterior painted by Mr. Emil Ernst
Costumes designed and made in Our Own Work Shop
Mr. Thomas Doyle, Sound Technician

Synopsis of Scenes for the Opera I PAGLIACCI

ACT I

An afternoon at the Crossroads near an Italian Village

10 minutes Intermission

ACT II

The same evening

No Encores until final curtain

Average performance running time ninety minutes
Ladies' and Gentlemen's lounge on second floor
Viking Lounge on Main Floor open during intermission

No smoking permitted in auditorium
Fire escape to right and left of stage
Not responsible for personal property unless
checked in Check Room

Theatre is Air Conditioned for your Comfort

The Danish Inscription
''EJ BLOT TIL LYST''
Which is over the Proscenium of the Royal Opera House in Copenhagen, Denmark, Means, in Translation
— — Not Only for Amusement — —

The Story

of

I PAGLIACCI
by Ruggiero Leoncavallo

THE PLOT

The scene of the story is laid in Calabria at the time of the Feast of the Virgin di Mezzagosto. During the prelude Tonio comes forward, as in the Prologue of ancient Greek tragedy, and explains that the subject of the play is taken from real life, and that the composer has devoted himself to expressing the sentiment, good or bad, but always human, of the characters he introduces. He then makes a sign for the curtain to rise.

ACT I

The first act shows the meeting of two roads at the entrance of a village; at the right a travelling theatre. Villagers greet the arrival of a troupe of strolling players. Canio, the Pagliaccio, and chief of the little troupe, invites the crowd to attend the performance at seven o'clock, and then goes off with Peppe (the *Harlequin)* and several peasants to drink at the tavern. Tonio, the *Clown,* remains behind to care for the donkey, but takes advantage of Canio's absence to declare his love to Nedda, who is the *Columbine* of the troupe, and also Canio's wife. Upon being pressed for a kiss she strikes Tonio and he goes off vowing to be revenged. Then Silvio, a rich young villager, joins Nedda and tries to induce her to leave her husband, and the forlorn life of a stroller, which she loathes, to run away with him. Tonio espies the lovers, and runs to fetch Canio. They return in time to hear Nedda's parting words to Silvio in which she agrees to meet him at night. Canio breaks from the restraining hands of Tonio to attack Silvio, but the latter succeeds in escaping without being recognized. Canio, baffled and jealous, orders Nedda to tell the name of her lover; but she refuses, and Canio is about to stab her, when Peppe interferes, persuades Nedda to go to the theatre to dress for her part, and induces Canio to be calm and prepare for the performance. The act closes with a cry of despair from Canio, who is obliged to act a comedy with death in his very soul, singing the famous aria "Vesti La Giubba".

ACT II

In the second act the peasants arrive to witness the performance. By chance this proves to be a burlesque of all that is taking place in the real life of the leading actors. Tonio, who plays the part of the idiot servant, makes a declaration of love to *Columbine,* (Nedda), which she receives with scorn. *Harlequin* (Peppe), in love with *Columbine,* then appears, but after a short interview is nearly surprised by the *Pagliaccio* (Canio), who arrives just as *Columbine* is helping *Harlequin* to run away, and hears her repeat to him the very words which she had used to Silvio when she bade him meet her after the play that night. At this Canio loses his head, forgets his part, and furiously demands the name of her lover. Nedda laughs in order to put the public off the scent, and they failing to grasp the truth, are much amused. Canio attempts to go on with the play; then suddenly, beside himself with rage and jealousy seizes the knife on the table and stabs Nedda to the heart, hoping that she will reveal the name of her lover with her last despairing cry. She calls to Silvio for help, and he attempts to reach her, but is attacked by Canio, who slays him also. The peasants disarm Canio, who exclaims, as if in a daze, "The comedy is finished."

Kungsholm
MINIATURE GRAND OPERA THEATRE'S
REPERTOIRE

AIDA   CARMEN   FAUST

    BARBER OF SEVILLE   TRISTAN and ISOLDE

                 DON GIOVANNI

OTELLO   MANON   MIKADO

    MADAME BUTTERFLY   HANSEL and GRETEL

                 DON PASQUALE

PAGLIACCI   LA BOHEME   RIGOLETTO

    LA TRAVIATA   TRIAL BY JURY

            CAVALLERIA RUSTICANA

MIGNON   LOUISE   WALKURE

    ORFEO ED EURIDICE   THE BARTERED BRIDE

            PELLEAS ET MELISANDE

    COSI FAN TUTTI   IL TROVATORE

                                      LA TOSCA

            SIEGFRED

*South Foyer to Grand Opera Theatre*_____

Mr. Chramer in the Control Room
Presenting Grand Opera

[1] Fredrik A. Chramer was born in Denmark in 1890. www.ancestry.com

[2] Drury, John, *Old Chicago Houses,* University of Chicago Press, 1941, p. 123.

[3] May 27, 1859 – February 2, 1934. www.ancestry.com

[4] Ibid.

[5] January 19, 1865 – June 26, 1938. www.ancestry.com

[6] www.usinflationcalculator.com

[7] www.lawry'salacart.com

[8] McKinney, Megan, "Deerings and McCormicks from the Beginning", *Classic Chicago Magazine,* n.d.

[9] Ibid.

[10] Ibid.

[11] www.usinflationcalculator.com

[12] Drury, John, *Old Chicago Houses,* University of Chicago Press, 1941, p. 123.

[13] Kungsholm Restaurant brochure, circa mid-1940's.

[14] Drury, John, *Old Chicago Houses,* University of Chicago Press, 1941, p. 110-123.

[15] Wolff, Ernest, "Why I'm Leaving International Banking to Play with Dolls", *The Chicago Guide,* Vol. 20, No. 7, July, 1971, p. 20

[16] By the early 1940's, Ernest spoke seven languages – English, French, German, Italian, Spanish, Portuguese, and Russian. *Michigan Times,* June 20, 1947, n.p.

[17] Ibid.

[18] "Kungsholm Miniature Grand Opera", *Puppetry Journal,* Vol.3 No. 3, p.6.

[19] Wolff, Ernest, "Why I'm Leaving International Banking to Play with Dolls", *The Chicago Guide,* Vol. 20, No. 7, July, 1971, p. 20.

[20] Ibid.

[21] Patent Application 2,327,234 filed November 22, 1942. Patent granted August 17, 1943.

[22] Putnam, Mabel Raef, "Puppet Opera", *Collier's*, March 10, 1945, p. 50.

[23] Email from Justin Snyder to author, November 4, 2018. Despite Chramer's preference, Mr. Snyder states he has yet to meet any woman who had worked as a Kungsholm puppeteer.

[24] "Stringless Puppets Put on Grand Opera", *Popular Mechanics*, March 1943, p. 14-15.

[25] Photograph of Kungsholm weekly repertoire listing.

[26] www.usinflationcalculator.com

[27] Legal documents in the Wolff archives, Chicago History Museum.

[28] Newspaper clippings in Esther Wolff's scrapbook. Chicago History Museum.

3 – **Fire**

AT 2:30 IN THE MORNING the morning of January 26, 1947, a fire broke out in the mansion's fourth floor theater. Chramer and his wife Katherine fled to the street from their apartment on the third floor. The fierce blaze burned for over an hour and a fireman had to be rescued by ladder from a window ledge when a wall of flames cut off his retreat.[1] The fire was confined to the top floor and it later was determined to have ignited in the area of the puppet stage. The entire floor was pretty much gutted and about half of the roof collapsed. All the puppets, costumes, scenery, props, stage, and lights were destroyed with damage estimated at $100,000 (over $1 million today[2]). In one newspaper account, Chramer claimed 1,500 puppets had been destroyed.[3]

A few months after the fire, Ernest won his lawsuit and Chramer was ordered to pay a settlement of $15,000 ($170,000. today[4]). In return he was granted a non-exclusive right to operate his version of the Wolffs' patented miniature opera.[5]

As the Wolffs continued touring in the Midwest, Esther Wolff was listed in the publicity and programs as "Mme. Theresa Wolff – Mistress of Puppeteers."[6] Her scrapbooks

Above: As the fire raged through the original miniature opera theatre on the mansion's fourth floor.

Right: The mansion's structural damage the next morning.

include numerous newspaper articles, photos and ads for the miniature opera's appearances. Some of the notices use the "Victor Puppet Opera" while a few others use the "American Puppet Opera."[7] To add further confusion, the names "Tivoli Grand Opera", "Puppet Opera Company", and "Ernest Wolff Puppet Opera" were also used in the later 1940's.

The only existing roster of company members is from July, 1947 and lists:

General Manager – Ward Caulle
Mistress of Puppeteers – Mme. Theresa Wolff
Administrative Assistant – Robert Takami
Stage Manager – Fritz Stoffer
Electrical Technician – Phillippe Brunet
Sound Technician – Dwight Sweet
Puppeteers – Virginia Bell, Miss Buckley, Eileen Nagatomo, Kyoko Oshima, Frances Whalen.
Custodian – Jeff Franks

In 1949, NBC television broadcast three of the Wolff operas: *Carmen* on Sunday May 15, *La Traviata*, on Tuesday, June 21, and *Aida* on Tuesday, June 28.[8] Two months later the Ernest Wolff Puppet Opera settled into the LaScala Room of the Hyde Park Hotel.[9]

With a company of thirteen people, the income did not cover all the expense and two months after opening at the Hyde Park Hotel, the entire Wolff inventory (six typewritten pages of puppets, props, lights, scenery, and equipment) were sold to Chramer for $6,500. ($69,000. today[10]). The Wolffs retired from puppet opera.[11]

Ernest entered the banking industry and in 1951 he married Sophie Fiske[12]. Twenty years later he retired as Second Vice President of the international banking department at the American National Bank and Trust of Chicago. However he did not completely abandon opera. During those years he produced and directed semi-professional operas in Chicago and New York, and he served several terms on Chicago's Lyric Opera Company Board of Directors.

After the fire, Chramer commissioned Everett Quinn and Associates to design a larger theater to be built on the eastern side of the mansion where the carriage house was located. An extension wrapped across the front and western sides of the mansion on the lawn between the mansion and the sidewalks on Ontario and Rush Streets. Behind this new façade was an enlarged restaurant lobby with a curving grand staircase to the second floor at the western end and a separate lobby to the new opera theater at the eastern end.

The new interiors were designed by Hanns Teichert, the same person who had created the Kungsholm Restaurant's original Swedish Modern interior. There is some confusion as to the inspiration for the Kungsholm auditorium. In some accounts the inspiration is the Royal Opera House in Copenhagen and in others, it is the Paris Opera House. Above the Kungsholm proscenium, which is similar to the Chicago Civic Opera House proscenium, is the slogan, "Ej Blot Til Lyst" ("Not Only for Amusement"). This was borrowed from the Royal Opera House in Copenhagen.

The new Kungsholm opera house was state-of-the-art. Above the 20' by 30' stage floor was a three-story fly loft for scenery. The control room, at the back of the auditorium boasted a complex board of autotransformers and switches to control the hundreds of stage lights, and the most up-to-date audio system. Each phonograph record was replaced after 82 performances because the sound quality deteriorated slightly each time the record was played.[13]

Kungsholm's new facade (circa 1952).
The top floor of the mansion, less the top cornice
is visible.

"Aida"
circa 1954

Pretty puppeteer poses on stage of the world's most elaborate puppet theater to show comparative size of tiny "actors" and the 52-piece "orchestra" in pit

The $500,000 Puppet Show

By Wayne Whittaker

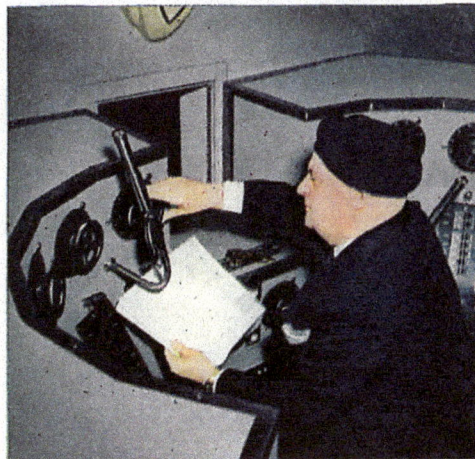

Fredrik A. Chramer, owner of the puppet theater, directs operas from the complicated control booth

MARVELS OF ELECTRONICS are combined with the ancient art of puppetry to give Chicago a truly unique puppet theater. The new miniature theater, which seats only 208 persons, is a medieval jewel box in red plush and gold with exquisite hand-painted murals and crystal chandeliers. Although the theater building is a separate unit, it adjoins and is operated in conjunction with a Swedish restaurant on Chicago's near north side.

Here full operas are given with recorded music and a retinue of more than 1700 specially built puppets—all on the grand scale of the New York Metropolitan or Paris opera houses. The puppets include a full 52-piece "orchestra" which occupies a pit in front of the 20-by-30-foot stage. When the lights dim, the orchestra pit is raised to stage level. A diminutive conductor,

Nadine Kangas, a puppeteer, displays the full cast of puppets which will be used in the opera *Rigoletto*

fondly nicknamed "Tosci" by the puppeteers, walks out, takes a bow, turns to his orchestra and lifts his baton. He leads the group in perfect tempo, and natural movements give an almost perfect illusion. The orchestra's movements are controlled backstage by a single lever, but Tosci is operated from below the stage by one of the eight puppeteers. It takes 15 persons behind the scenes to put on an opera, including stage directors, scenery and wardrobe personnel, and one or two persons in the control booth located above the miniature balcony.

This control booth with its semicircular instrument panel, sound equipment, microphones, switches, dials and flashing lights resembles nothing more than the cockpit of a B-29 bomber. The "pilot" occupies a seat before a window that gives him a perfect view of the stage. He is almost encircled by the control board. From here he controls all sound reproduction and the elaborate lighting equipment, which consists of footlights with 620 small bulbs, proscenium border lights with 1240 bulbs, flood border lights with 112 bulbs, 20 miniature spotlights with 100-watt bulbs and two 20-footlong cyclorama blue lights with 75-watt bulbs.

The director is in constant touch by wireless intercom with the puppeteers, who

Cutaway painting of the theater shows puppeteers at work beneath slotted stage during *Madame Butterfly* performance. Below are workrooms and storage space

Jewel-box interior of the puppet theater, which seats 208 persons, is like a miniature grand-opera house

must work in cramped space under the stage. The opera puppets are not like marionettes, which are operated by strings from above. They are rigid puppets supported from below by rods and controlled by wires with rings on the ends which fit the puppeteers' fingers. The stage floor has row after row of horizontal slots along which the puppets move and a bisecting center slot enabling them to move from one row to another and to the front or rear of the stage.

The puppeteers sit on low stools equipped with rollers which enable them to scoot

Johannes Foerster studies each puppet after performance and dabs make-up paint where it's needed

To pick up their cues, puppeteers working below the stage wear headphones which are plugged into stools

silently about beneath the slotted floor. Occasionally there may be a collision at the height of some complicated operatic mob scene, but usually all runs smoothly after weeks of rehearsal. The stools are specially equipped to pick up impulses from wires built into the floor. All operators wear headphones plugged into the stools and the transmission of their cues from the control booth is similar to the operation of a walkie-talkie radio. Microphones are located under the stage so the puppeteers can talk back to the booth. Their voices come into the booth through a loudspeaker.

During a recent evening performance, a puppeteer's headphones snagged a wire connected to a bouquet which was being carried carefully by a puppet on the stage. The bouquet whisked through a slot in the floor in a jiffy. After a moment of subdued hilarity among the puppeteers, the bouquet obligingly rose through the floor and back into the hands of Suzuki, the maid of Madame Butterfly.

The headphones of the puppeteers pick up the opera music and singing along with the director's cues. Eventually all 17 operas will be recorded on a four-track tape so they can be fed simultaneously into the electronic control board, which will transmit only the music and singing to the theater auditorium; the music and singing plus cues into the headphones of the puppeteers; and the music and lighting directions for all scenes to the director in the booth.

One of the greatest tributes guests pay to the little opera occurs after a performance when they ask if the puppets are three or four feet high. Actually they are only 13 inches high but everything in the stage settings is in such perfect proportion that the puppets seem much larger. A great deal of the scenery, which is all built in the theater's own workshop backstage, is patterned after that of the Metropolitan Opera. The theater now owns 340 pieces of scenery for settings, which include street scenes, gardens, palaces, Japanese pagodas, bridges, forests, mountains and churches. Elaborate backdrops and other stage effects are lowered from a fly loft three stories high. The rigging ropes and weights could support the heavy settings of a normal-size theater, according to Fredrik A. Chramer, the owner.

In many scenes where the action is simple and the lighting subdued, this miniature opera creates a complete illusion of reality —a triumph of electronics and hard work.

★ ★ ★

¶Emphasizing the growing complexity of aircraft, more than three million hours of engineering time were required to design the latest U. S. Air Force bomber.

SEPTEMBER 1952

Above: Fredrik Charmer in the control booth with the new ¼" tape recorders which replaced the phonograph playback system.

The sound technician's task was often more difficult than seamlessly switching from one record to the next. Sometimes a well-known American operatic star, such as Lily Pons or Lawrence Tibbit, would be cut into an opera to sing a famous aria. With the introduction of ¼" audio tape recording, the phonograph records were transferred to tape – a change which eliminated deteriorating sound quality as well as having to switch records during the performance. And a featured star's arias could easily be edited into the audio tape.

A wireless intercom system enabled the puppeteers, who wore earphones under the stage, to hear the directions from Chramer who was in the control booth on the balcony at the back of the auditorium.

The auditorium was described as a "jewel box" of 208 red plush seats, gold trim, and murals on the walls, two elevated boxes on the side mural-decorated walls, a narrow balcony with the control room behind, and an elaborate crystal chandelier.

Edward N. Nelson of Oak Park was commissioned to make new puppets which were then painted, wigged, and costumed in the theater workshop. The elaborate sets, scale props, and small furniture were created in the well-equipped workshop on the mansion's fourth floor in what had been the original theater. All the operas destroyed by the fire were rebuilt until the Kungsholm Miniature Grand Opera repertoire totaled 25 operas.[14]

The diminutive orchestra conductor was a distinguished white-haired, tuxedo wearing chap who became a member of Chicago's social elite. In the spring when his black jacket was exchanged for a white summer coat, and again in the fall when he changed back to black, the event was mentioned in newspaper social columns.[15]

Tosci

By the mid-1950's, Chramer's health began to falter as he dealt with growing financial problems. In 1957 he leased the Kungsholm operation to the 'Fred Harvey' company and retired. The lease included a clause requiring the puppet opera to continue operating.[16]

After several strokes, Fredrik A. Chramer died on July 7, 1960.[17]

Manipulating puppets from
beneath the slotted floor.

Kungsholm
MINIATURE GRAND OPERA THEATRE · CHICAGO

Souvenir Program

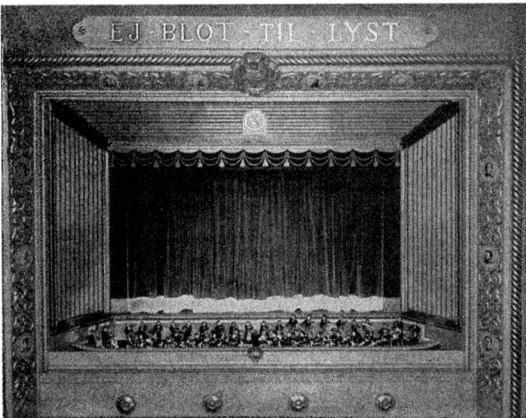

FOLLOWING the disastrous fire which occurred in February, 1947, destroying my miniature Puppet Opera, I have now been able to again open in a very modern theatre, therefore this evening you have been invited as my guests, to the Kungsholm Miniature Grand Opera Theatre created for the pleasure of my guests and friends who like it and I hope you too will enjoy the performance which I have planned for you as much as I enjoy having you here; therefore I would greatly appreciate my guests refraining from conversation or leaving the auditorium during the performance, as it may disturb the audience.

Fine Operas and good music are my hobbies and have been for many years (in fact I presented my first Puppet Opera to my schoolmates when I was nine years of age); from them I have gained not only limitless pleasures, but relaxation from business as well; consequently my approach in building this Opera Theatre has realized my life long dream and has been a personal one for the joy and satisfaction it gives, also an outlet for creative instincts.

This Opera House has been built to bring forth the true picture of the fine Operas which the Victor, as well as the Columbia Recording Companies have so successfully produced from the two great Opera Companies La Scala, Milan and L'Opera Paris-France. Guest artists all via recording, such as Lauritz Melchior, Kirsten Flagstad, Lotte Lehmann, Pons, Bjoerling, John Charles Thomas, Steber, Albanese, Dorothy Kirsten, Sayao, Peerce, Tucker and Leonard Warren are heard during some of the performances.

To present my repertoire of twenty-four operas, the Victor and Columbia Musical masterpiece albums which I have in my music library are reproduced by the latest R.C.A. commercial transcription tables and transferred over to custom built professional tape recorders made by the Ampex Electric Corporation of Redwood City, California, and then brought to the auditorium through Jensen's Loudspeakers.

A personnel of fifteen people are required to perform the numerous understage and backstage operations including manipulating of the stringless puppets, operating the electric control board (which by the way was built by Hubb Electric Company of Chicago), and the sound system, shifting scenery between acts, changing costumes, wigs and make-up; the seventeen hundred puppets (which are thirteen inches in height) who sing, dance, love, fight and die in my opera productions are operated from below the twenty by thirty foot stage by twelve trained operators who are music students and know each opera note for note.

An extensive wardrobe consisting of more than eighteen hundred opera costumes is required, supplemented by hats, wigs, silk stockings, shirts, silk tights, aprons, boots and shoes. Each costume is an exact copy (in miniature) of those worn by Metropolitan and La Scala opera artists. All of the new puppets and costumes which we now possess have been created and built in our own work shop.

Three hundred forty pieces of scenery and set-pieces include street scenes, gardens, palaces, interiors, a bull arena, mountains, forest, a prison, houses, stairways, bedrooms, churches, brick walls, rocks, bridges, etcetera.

The lighting equipment consists of foot lights with six hundred twenty small bulbs, four proscenium border lights with twelve hundred forty small bulbs, five flood border lights with one hundred twelve—seventy-five watt bulbs, twenty miniature spot lights with one hundred watt bulbs and two—twenty foot long cyclorama blue lights also with seventy-five watt bulbs.

The chandelier seen in the first act of La Traviata was constructed from genuine Czecho-Slovakian crystal, while the one in the third act is of brass and has forty-four candelabra lights.

The fly loft is three stories high with rigging of eighteen border lines, and in the orchestra pit a full size Opera Orchestra of fifty-two puppets is complete with violins, cellos, bass violins, harps, clarinets, flutes, french horns, bassoons, kettle drums and other orchestral instruments. The diminutive conductor "Tosci" leads the Puppet musicians in perfect tempo with the music.

Stage properties comprise a fine collection of miniatures and consist of six complete suites of period furniture, spinning wheel, tables, chairs, fireplaces, clocks, vases, candlesticks, plates, jewel boxes, couches, lanterns, chandeliers, donkey carts, love seats and many other pieces, most of which are produced in my own work shop.

The Opera Building was designed by the great architects Everett F. Quinn and Associates of Chicago, according to my own ideas. The interior decorating was done by the famous artist, Mr. Hanns R. Teichert, who also did the interior decorating of the Kungsholm Restaurant. The murals are by the great artist, Frank A. Lackner.

I take great pleasure in mentioning the above firms and publicly thank them for displaying such outstanding interest in helping me to create this modern miniature Opera House.

Permit me also at this time to thank you, my guests, for your valuable patronage at the Kungsholm, and I wish to extend to you and your guests the invitation to be present at a performance in my home Miniature Opera House any evening soon.

Fredrik A. Cramer
Founder

KUNGSHOLM MINIATURE GRAND OPERA

(Created for my guests and friends who like it)

FREDRIK A. CHRAMER
Founder and General Director

KARL LAUFKOTTER
(Former tenor Metropolitan Opera Company of New York for eleven years)
Assistant to Mr. Chramer

PRESENTS

HANSEL AND GRETEL

Fairy Opera in Three Acts

by

ENGELBERT HUMPERDINCK

(Libretto by Adelheid Wette after the fairy tale by Grimm)
(Sung in English)

CHARACTERS IN ORDER OF APPEARANCE

GRETEL	NADINE CONNER
HANSEL	RISE STEVENS
THE MOTHER	CLARAMAE TURNER
THE FATHER	JOHN BROWNLEE
THE SANDMAN	THELMA VOTIPKA
THE DEW FAIRY	LILLIAN RAYMONDI
THE WITCH	THELMA VOTIPKA

Angels and Enchanted Children

Orchestra and Chorus of the
METROPOLITAN OPERA COMPANY
Conducted by MAX RUDOLF

Kungsholm Miniature Opera Conductor "Tosci"

Scenery after Fredrik A. Chramer's ideas
Designed by Karl Laufkotter

Staged and directed by Frederick A. Chramer

Scenery built and painted in our Work Shop

Costumes by Jack Hakman

Thomas Doyle, Sound Technician and Prompter

SYNOPSIS OF SCENES

ACT I	ACT II
The Broommaker's Cottage	A Forest Near the Cottage

ACT III
The Witch's House

Running time of this performance
is approximately two hours.

Ladies' and Gentlemen's lounge downstairs.

Viking lounge on Main Floor open during
intermission.

No smoking permitted in entire Theatre Building.
Fire exits to right and left of stage.

Not responsible for personal property
unless checked in Check Room.

Theatre is Air Conditioned for your Comfort

The Story of

HANSEL AND GRETEL

ACT I — The Broommaker's Cottage

In a cottage in the woods lives Peter the broommaker and his wife Gertrude with their two children Hansel and Gretel. The father and mother are away selling brooms and the children are performing their duties about the cottage. They soon become tired of their tasks and begin to dance and play. At this moment the mother enters and scolds them for not working, and when she goes to punish them she knocks a jug of milk from the table which was their evening meal. In her anger she sends the children out to the woods to pick strawberries and warns them not to come back until their baskets are full. The father enters in a joyful mood. He tells his wife he has sold all of his brooms at the fair and shows her a basket filled with provisions. When he learns that Hansel and Gretel have been sent into the forest he becomes alarmed and reminds his wife they are in danger of a witch who lives there. The parents rush out to look for their children.

ACT II — A Forest Near the Cottage

Hansel and Gretel are wandering through the forest. While Hansel picks the strawberries, Gretel sits under a tree and sings. The children then sit down with the basket of berries and eat them until all are gone. Night begins to fall and they want to leave the forest, but have lost their way. The woods are now filled with ghostly sounds and shadows which frighten them. The Sandman arrives, sprinkles sleep into their eyes and sings them a lullaby. When he leaves the children say their prayers and fall asleep. A stairway appears from the skies and angels descend to protect the sleeping children.

ACT III — The Witch's House

The Dew Fairy comes to wake Hansel and Gretel. They tell their dreams to each other. Then suddenly they see a little house made of candy and gingerbread. The children begin nibbling at the house, when the Witch comes out. She tells them not to be afraid, and as they start to run away she fixes them to the spot with her magic wand. She then locks Hansel in a cage to get him fat and orders Gretel to do her housework, then dances wildly around on a broom while the frightened children watch. Gretel steals the magic wand and frees Hansel from the cage. The Witch now orders Gretel to look in the oven to see if the cakes are ready. Gretel asks the Witch to show her how, and as the Witch stoops before the oven the children shove her inside and slam the door. They dance and sing with joy. With a loud crash the oven falls apart and all the captive children are freed from their gingerbread form. Peter and Gertrude, who have been searching the woods all night, arrive and all sing a song of thanksgiving.

The Danish Inscription
"EJ BLOT TIL LYST"
Which is over the Proscenium of the Royal Opera House in
Copenhagen, Denmark, means in translation,
"NOT ONLY FOR AMUSEMENT"

Kungsholm
MINIATURE GRAND OPERA REPERTOIRE

AIDA • LA TRAVIATA • CAVALLERIA RUSTICANA • IL TROVATORE

RIGOLETTO • CARMEN • FAUST • NORMA • LA BOHEME • LOHENGRIN

PAGLIACCI • LA TOSCA • SALOME • TURANDOT • WALKURE

TRISTAN AND ISOLDE • MADAME BUTTERFLY • HANSEL AND GRETEL

LUCIA DI LAMMERMOOR • TANNHAUSER • TRIAL BY JURY

My first Opera Theatre at age of nine

OPENING NIGHT
Mrs. Lauritz Melchior Congratulates Mr. Chramer
On His Miniature Grand Opera Achievement

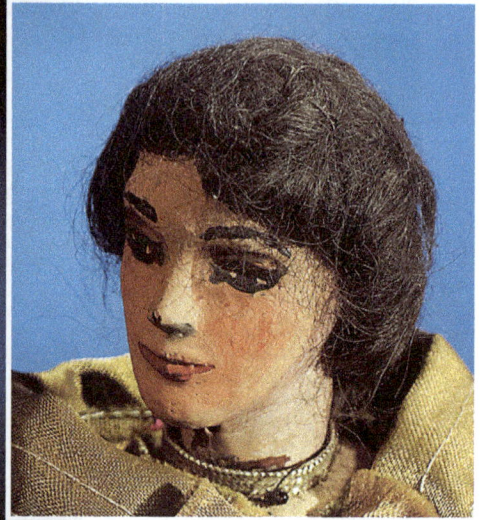

Chorus member

"La Boheme"

Chorus member

"Student Prince"

Chorus member

"La Boheme"

Lieutenant Pinkerton

"Madame Butterfly"

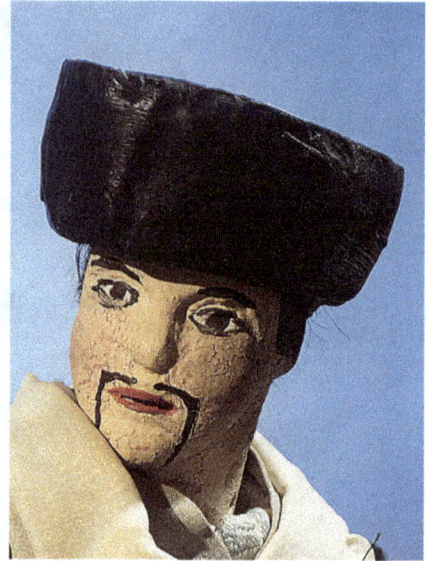

The Bonze

"Madame Butterfly"

(Unidentified)

Canio

"Pagliacci"

Chorus member

"Hansel & Gretel"

[1] *Chicago Daily News*, January 26, 1947, n.p.

[2] www.inflationcalculator.com

[3] *Chicago Daily News*, January 26, 1947. n.p.

[4] Wolff Archives at Chicago History Museum

[5] Wolff, Ernest, "Why I'm Leaving International Banking to Play with Dolls", *The Chicago Guide*, Vol. 20, No. 7, July, 1971, p. 20

[6] *Grand Rapids Press*, July 8, 1947, n/p.

[7] Chicago History Museum.

[8] Undated production notes in the Wolff archives.

[9] *Chicago Sun-Times*, April 7, 1949, n/p.

[10] www.inflationcalculator.com

[11] Typewritten inventory dated October 20, 1949.

[12] 1910 – 1999, www.ancestry.com

[13] *Chicago Sun-Times*, April 22, 1971, n.p.

[14] *Progress* Museum of Science and Industry, May-June, 1982, n.p.

[15] Morrison, Julie, "The Kungsholm Miniature Grand Opera Theatre", University of Connecticut, 1997.

[16] *Chicago Sun-Times*, April 22, 1971, n.p.

[17] www.ancestry.com

4 – Fred Harvey
Kungsholm Curtain Descends

THE COMPANY who took over the Kungsholm operation had nearly a century of experience in the food service industry. In 1878 Fred Harvey began to assemble a chain of restaurants along the Atchison, Topeka, and Santa Fe Railroad's main line from Kansas City into the southwest. At the time, steam locomotives had to stop about every one hundred miles for water and fuel. During the thirty-minute layover, passengers would rush to the station's restaurant for a quick meal before the train continued its journey. As these station restaurants were locally operated, the quality of food, service, and cleanliness varied – mostly from bad to worse. The restaurants Fred Harvey established offered well-prepared quality food, reasonable prices, prompt service by a staff of well-trained young waitresses known as "Harvey Girls", and spotless premises.

When the company was incorporated, the registered name was 'Fred Harvey', not 'Fred Harvey and Sons' or 'Fred Harvey Company.'[1] 'Fred Harvey' expanded to include railway dining cars and newsstands then when automobiles, improved roads, and the Great Depression reduced railroad passengers, 'Fred Harvey' began catering to tourists. The El Tovar Hotel on the rim of the Grand Canyon was built

Above: Fred Harvey
Below: Company Logo

and operated for many years by the company. By the 1950's 'Fred Harvey' began opening oasis-stop restaurants along the nation's new tollways and freeways and it began to acquire a few high class restaurants such as the Kungsholm Scandinavian Restaurant in Chicago.

In 1957, Fredrik Chramer signed a twenty-five year lease for 'Fred Harvey' to take over the Kungsholm Swedish Restaurant. The agreement stipulated the miniature opera had to be continued. However, without Chramer's constant supervision, the quality of food in the restaurant began to slide and without his enthusiastic vision, the opera's energy began to fade. William Fosser, who had worked in the theater as a lad in the early 1940's and again in the early 1950's, was hired to direct the opera theater but after three years and a dispute with the restaurant management, Fosser left and the theater's decline resumed.[2] More and more operas in the repertoire were replaced by staged concert versions of Broadway musicals. Unlike the operas, the musicals were only the characters performing to the songs on the original cast albums. None of the spoken dialogue or scene actions were included although occasionally a narrative of the storyline was included to bridge the recorded songs.[3]

Then in 1968 'Fred Harvey' was acquired by Amfac Inc., a land development company in Hawaii who were expanding into the food service industry.[4] The decline of the Kungsholm Scandinavian Restaurant and its after-dinner Miniature Grand Opera accelerated until 1971 when the entire operation was closed.[5]

Realizing Chicago had lost a cultural gem, the public and several newspaper columnists expressed concern. Newspaper columnist Jack Schinedler wrote, "Most of the 1,700 puppets, who were carved and assembled years ago by a local craftsman named Edward Nelson, are moldering in an upstairs storeroom."[6]

Paul Taber, vice president of the Fred Harvey branch of Amfac responded, "Times change and no one seemed to care about puppets in recent years. The theater cost us $6,000 ($37,000.00[7] today) per month, and nobody came to see the damn thing."[8]

Kathe Mazer, assistant to the producer of the short-lived theater company with some of the Kungsholm puppets in their storage case.

Ernest Wolff had just retired from banking when he read Taber's response. He offered to take over the Kungsholm opera theater and assume full financial, artistic, and administrative responsibility.[9] However Amfac rebranded the restaurant as Shipwreck Kelly's and the opera theater was converted to a theater with live actors. Both the restaurant and theater received poor reviews and closed within a few months. The premises were then leased to Lawry's, the Los Angeles-based seasoned salt company who were expanding their steak houses across the country.

In a two year construction project, the restaurant's public rooms were restored to an 1890 appearance and the jewel opera theater was converted to an additional dining room. A level floor was installed above the auditorium's sloping floor and extended over the slotted floor. The stage area became a cozy alcove to the main room but behind its walls, ceiling, and floor are the remains of the miniature opera stage house. Beneath the restaurant's floor is the slotted puppet stage floor and four feet below that is the level floor where the puppeteers rolled around on low stools while operating the figures. Beneath that level is the basement where puppets were stored in special cabinets and the stage crew gathered in the "Green Room."

Lawry's The Prime Rib, which is still at the same location, occasionally conducts tours through the backstage area.

Left: Kungsholm theater during renovation

Below Left: Lawry's The Prime Rib dining room

Below Right: Dining alcove in the former stage area.

When the Kungsholm Miniature Grand Opera was closed, the puppets, scenery, props, and costumes were left in the basement beneath the stage where they were plundered by people working in the building. William Fosser later said, "I'm not surprised that as many as 1,000 are gone. The puppets were thrown in piles downstairs. Anybody could have taken them."[10]

The basement area was subject to flooding whenever there was heavy rain so scenery, props, and puppets left on the floor began to rot and fall apart.

Looking up from the
basement to
the floor where
the puppeteers
operated the puppets.
Through the slots of the
stage floor can be
glimpsed the
floor of the
dining room alcove.

Right: The former puppet
storage and Green Room in the
basement below the
puppeteers' floor.

A quintet of
orchestra musicians
waiting to practice.

The construction of an office tower on the north side of the building destabilized the original mansion in 1984, and the top two floors had to be removed. The street façade remained unaltered.

The building had been purchased by the Grossinger family and one day Rose and Sharon Grossinger discovered a number of puppets were entombed in an unlocked basement room. The puppets stored in boxes were in better condition than those just piled around the room and the Grossingers donated the small figures to the Museum of Science and Industry where a few were exhibited from October 27, 1977 to March 26, 1978.[11]

For four years the museum tried to raise the money to create a permanent exhibit. Although the finances were still about 60% below the budget, the museum decided to go ahead as best they could.[12] Some fifty of the battered, shop-worn Kungsholm puppets were restored and a four-minute computerized animated sequence of the Gypsy Dance in Act 4 of "Carmen" was created. While it played, a simultaneous video was showing of the same scene performed by the Vienna State Opera. Another display detailed how the puppets were created and operated.[12]

In recognition of the exhibit, the 1986 Puppeteers of America Award was presented jointly to the Museum of Science and Industry and to the Illinois Federation of Women's Clubs who had raised a sizeable portion of the needed financing.[13]

William Fosser's Opera in Focus was hired to perform in the museum's Little Theater on weekends and holidays through the first summer. Fosser later said the exhibit lacked the human element, "A puppet is an instrument of expression like a musical instrument. The exhibit is totally mechanical, no more like real puppetry than the animated store window displays at Christmas."[14]

The "permanent" exhibit closed on June 17, 2002, and the 300-odd puppets were returned to the Kungsholm build-

Three of the Kungsholm Miniature Grand Opera performers exhibited at the Swedish American Museum in 2018.

ing where they remained until 2017 when Rose Grossinger donated them to the Swedish American Museum. In September, 2018, the museum opened an exhibit of these puppets and when it closed in November, the figures went back into storage – this time at the Swedish American Museum.

Aside from the Kungsholm puppets now at the Swedish American Museum, only a handful of others are known to exist. The Cook/Marks Collection in Seattle, the Puppetry Arts Center in Atlanta, the Ballard Institute and Museum of Puppetry in Storrs CT, and Lawry's The Prime Rib have only a couple dozen between them. Very few of the missing puppets have ever been offered for sale.

The Fred Harvey management of the Kungsholm restaurant is delighted to be able to continue, virtually without change, the popular miniature grand opera. Conceived by Mr. Fredrik A. Chramer, founder of the Kungsholm, for the pleasure and entertainment of his friends and guests, the puppet opera has become a Chicago institution.

The development of this miniature grand opera theater brought Mr. Chramer himself a great deal of pleasure, since it helped to satisfy a life-long interest in good music. The present facilities, constructed anew after the original puppets and theater were destroyed by fire in 1947, contain the finest sound equipment available.

Through special reproducing arrangements with both Victor and Columbia we are able to bring you the recorded works of the opera companies La Scala, the Paris Opera and the Metropolitan. Guest artists, also recorded of course, include such stars as Licia Albanese, Erna Berger, Jussi Bjoerling, Maria Callas, Boris Christoff, Nicolai Gedda, Beniamino Gigli, Tito Gobbi, Victoria de los Angeles, Robert Merrill, Jan Peerce, Eleanor Steber, Giuseppe di Stefano, Rise Stevens, Italo Tajo, Renata Tebaldi, Richard Tucker and Leonard Warren.

A staff of as many as ten people is required to manage the many understage and backstage operations such as handling the stringless puppets, shifting scenery and changing costumes and make-up. The "resident company" numbers seventeen hundred puppets, each approximately thirteen inches high.

The miniature wardrobe includes more than eighteen hundred costumes, supplemented by hats, wigs, boots and other accessories. Three hundred and forty pieces of scenery and set pieces are available and are scaled to suit the twenty-foot by thirty-foot stage. The fly loft is three stories high. The orchestra pit is staffed with fifty-two puppets led by the diminutive "Tosci."

Nearly all of the scenery, costumes and properties, as well as the puppets themselves, were made in the Kungsholm workrooms under the personal direction of Mr. Chramer.

Interior decorating of the theater was done by Hanns R. Teichert, who also did the decorating in the restaurant. Murals are by the well-known Frank A. Lackner. The inscription "EJ BLOT TIL LYST" appears originally over the proscenium of the Royal Opera House in Copenhagen. It means, "NOT ONLY FOR AMUSEMENT."

Kungsholm Miniature Opera Repertoire

La Boheme ✱ I Pagliacci ✱ Rigoletto
Carmen ✱ Trial by Jury
Cavalleria Rusticana ✱ Hansel and Gretel

Die Walkure ✱ Tosca ✱ La Traviata
Faust ✱ H. M. S. Pinafore
Madame Butterfly ✱ The Elixir of Love

WEEKDAY PERFORMANCES:
Mon. through Fri. 8 PM; Sat. 2 PM, 8 PM and 10:15 PM; Wed. also 2 PM. Guests are requested to arrive about 2 hours before curtain time.

SUNDAY PERFORMANCES:
Sunday afternoon at 3 PM; Sunday evening at 8 PM. Guests are requested to arrive about 2 hours before curtain time.

Reservations recommended — WHitehall 4-2700

Above: Puppet display in Lawry's The Prime Rib

Below: Box of assorted puppet parts

Chorus member

"Hansel & Gretel"

(Unidentified)

Both pages

(Unidentified)

Possibly from *"Carmen"*

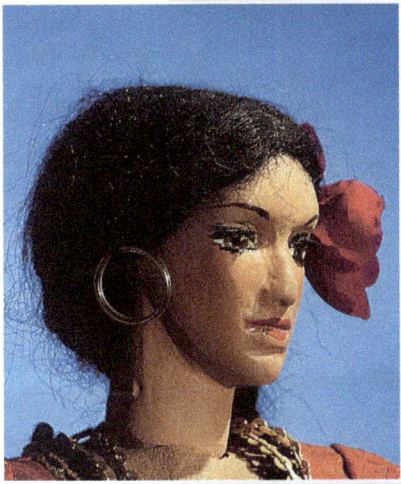

(Unidentified)

Possibly from *"Carmen"*

(Unidentified)
Possibly Mallika
from *"Lakmé"*

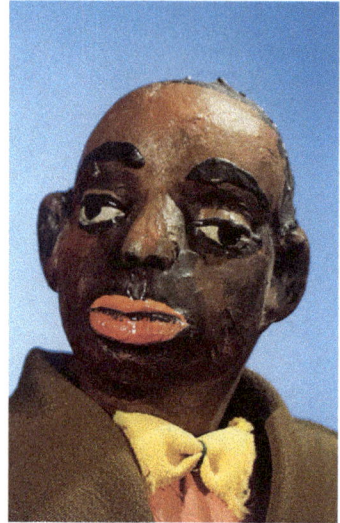

Lawyer Frazier

"Porgy & Bess"

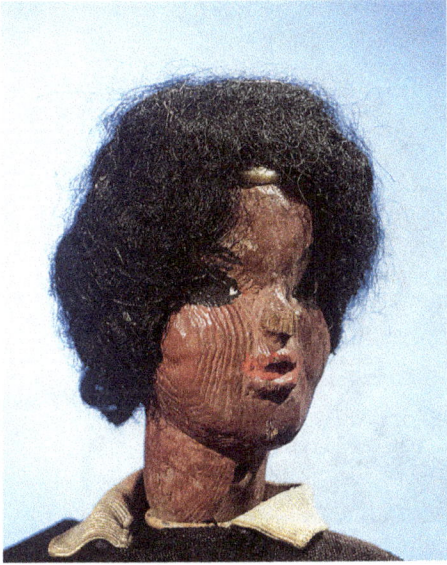

Chorus member

"Porgy & Bess"

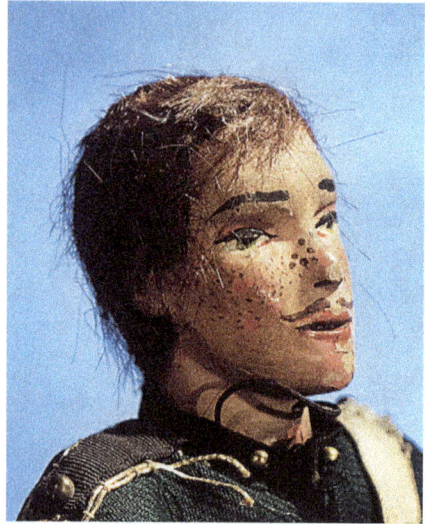

Chorus member

"Student Prince"

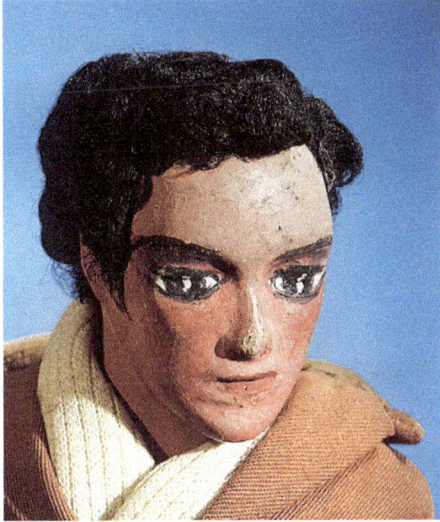

(Unidentified)

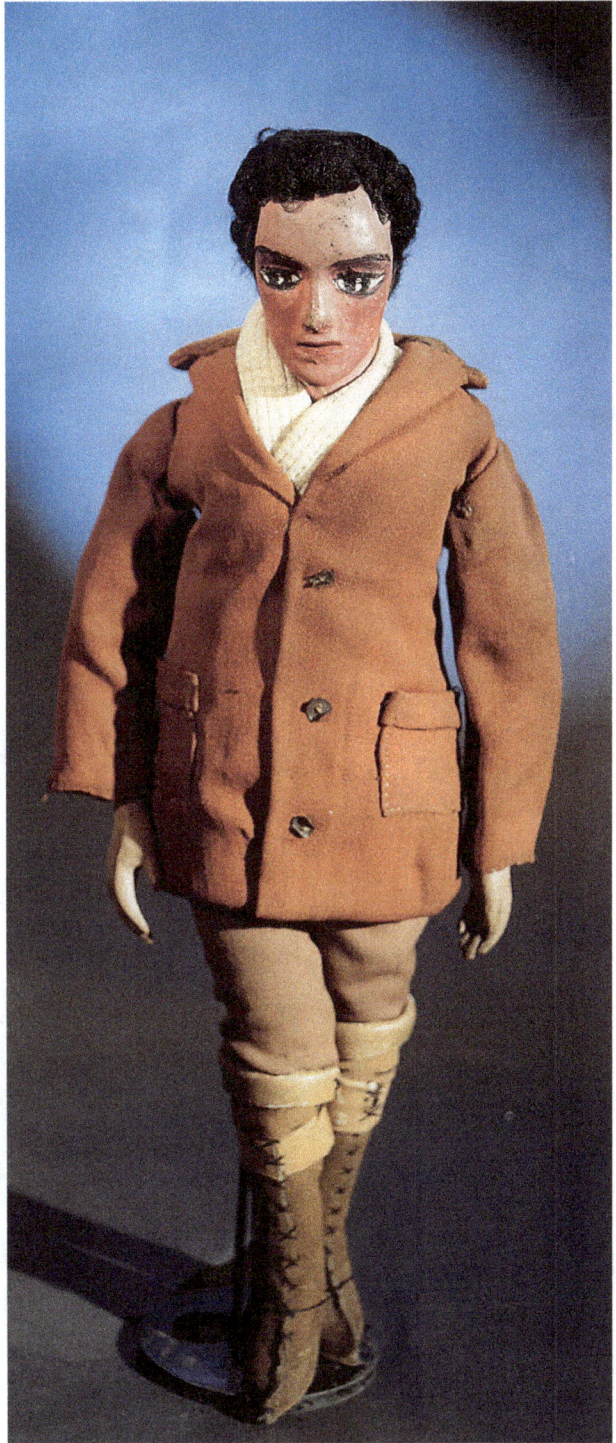

Chorus member

"Sound of Music"

Chorus member

"Sound of Music"

(Unidentified)

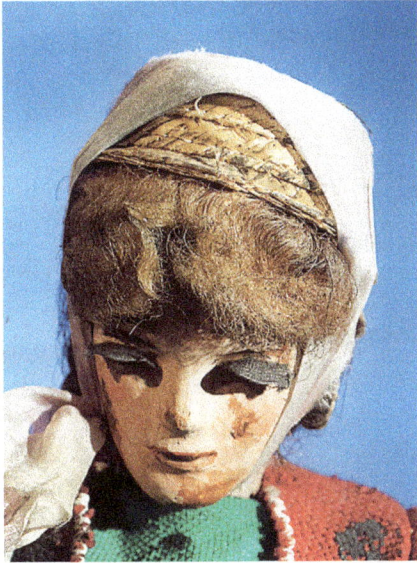

Eliza Doolittle

"My Fair Lady"

[1] Fried, Stephen, *Appetite for America*, Bantam Books, New York, 2010, p. xvii.

[2] Jones, Gary, *Subplot: Memoirs of the Kungsholm Miniature Grand Opera*, Charlemagne Press, Garden Bay, BC, Canada, 2018, p. 66.

[3] Email to Author from Gary Jones, January 26, 2019.

[4] https://en.wikipedia.org/wiki/

[5] *À la Carte*, Lawry's Restaurants newsletter, 1974, p. 2.

[6] Schinedler, Jack, "What Became of the Puppet Opera?" *Panorama – Chicago Daily News* July 6-7, 1974, p. 3.

[7] www.usinflationcalculator.com.

[8] Letter: Paul Taber to *Chicago Daily News*, n.d., n.p.

[9] Letter: Ernest Wolff to Paul Taber, June 17, 1971.

[10] "Permanent Exhibit Creates a Home for 'Forsaken' Kungsholm Puppets." *Progress*, Museum of Science and Industry, May-June, 1982. n.p.

[11] *Sunday Sun-Times*, April 18, 1982, p. 2.

[12] "Puppet Opera: Grand Opera on a Miniature Scale', *Progress*, Museum of Science and Industry, July-August, 1981, n.p.

[13] *2007-2008 Hand Book and Directory*, Puppeteers of America, p. 60.

[14] Chamberlain, Charles, "Chicago's famed Kungsholm Puppets perform once more", *Alton Telegraph*, May 14, 1982, p. A-2.

5 – **William Fosser**
Opera in Focus

ALL THREE IMPRESARIOS of Chicago's miniature opera companies were introduced to opera at a young age. Ernest Wolff was twelve, Fredrik Chramer was nine, and William Fosser[1], who founded Opera in Focus, was seven when he saw *"Il Trovatore"* by Fortune Gallo's itinerant San Carlos Opera.[2]

In 1940 an aunt gave him a copy of Ruth Vickery Holmes' *Model Theater Craft: Scenery, Actors, and Plays* which details the construction of a model theater. Unlike regular model theaters which use flat paper figures operated from the stage wings, the Holmes' theater had simple characters made from pipe cleaners and moved from beneath a slotted floor.[3]

When Fosser was fourteen, a newspaper photo of a girl holding an armful of Kungsholm rod puppets inspired him to apply to work at the Kungsholm. He was immediately hired as a backstage assistant when Chramer saw examples of Fosser's work. But five months later, Fosser's parents forced him to quit because his school grades were suffering.[4]

After Fosser graduated from high school, his father agreed to pay half the tuition at the Goodman Theater's acclaimed School of Drama provided Fosser earned the rest. He became a window dresser at Marshall Fields until he'd earned the needed $400.00 ($5,600 today[5]). After only the first year, he

William B. Fosser
with Giaconda

quit the prestigious theater school because the teaching staff were withholding their services in a labor dispute and classes were being taught by the assistants.[6]

Fosser worked for a brief time in Ernest Wolff's new company but when the new Kungsholm Miniature Grand Opera theatre was preparing to open, Ernest Wolff withdrew from miniature operas. Fosser returned to the Kungsholm and stayed for three years before he began working in films where the pay was so much better. Finally he was able to commission the Dick Rush Company to cast thirty metal bases from the design he had been refining for over a decade. Each figure cost $650.00[7] ($6,130.00 today[8]) – plus the wigging, costume, and finishing.

During his time at the Kungsholm, Fosser realized puppets, with their limited movement, did not adequately sustain a full-length opera so he decided to stage individual arias and short scenes rather than entire operas.[9] The concentration on individual arias led to the name "Opera in Focus" which in turn generated the idea of the theatre's circular proscenium resembling a camera lens. The proscenium has been modified to a semi-circular opening behind a traditional rectangular proscenium.

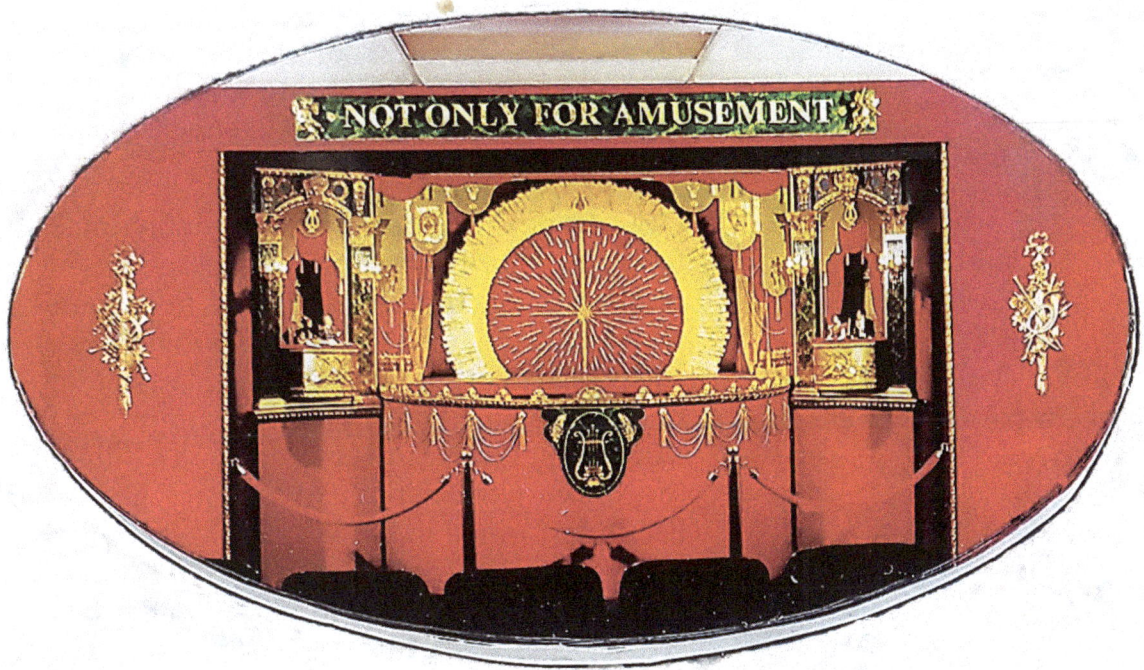

Opera in Focus proscenium

Opera in Focus was officially launched in 1955 in a rented storefront theater. After about a year, the theater closed[10] and Fosser returned to film work where he was establishing a reputation as an outstanding art director and set designer. Over the years, he worked on films such as: *"Home Alone," "Ordinary People," "The Breakfast Club," "Groundhog Day," "A League of Their Own,"* and many others.

In 1961, he applied for a patent of his basic puppet design. The patent was not registered until 1968 because the application was modified several times.

Opera in Focus moved to the Impresario Restaurant in Detroit in 1961 but the restaurant closed after only a year[11] so Fosser returned to Chicago and film work. In 1964 he was appointed Artistic Director at the Kungsholm Miniature Grand Opera.[12] Three years later his final production for

One of Fosser's
puppets for the Kungsholm
production of "Kismet"

the Kungsholm was a staged concert version of *"Kismet"* which used his rod puppets rather than Wolff figures. According to later backstage gossip, Fosser was fired and banned from the theater.[13]

Over the next two decades, Fosser attempted to establish Opera in Focus in Chicago's cultural scene. He tried several times to emulate the Kungsholm's after-dinner opera theater at such restaurants as the Victorian House and the Magic Pan.[14] During the first summer of the Kungsholm Miniature Grand Opera exhibit at the Museum of Science and Industry, Opera in Focus performed in the Museum's little theater. Audiences were small because people couldn't find the theater which was tucked into an obscure corner of the immense building. A tour of Midwest schools was attempted, and even the Epcot Center in Florida expressed interest in the company, although nothing came of it. In 1979 Fosser was offered space at Niles College Seminary but regular public performances were not permitted because of the insurance restrictions.[15] For the next ten years, the puppets and equipment were stored there, while Fosser continued to improve and expand the repertoire.

Fosser was diagnosed with cancer in 1979 and his left lung was removed,[16] yet he continued to build and refine his productions and search for a permanent home for his beloved miniature opera. He joined a consortium of artists to create a children's arts center in Park Ridge but after two years of planning and fund raising, the project fell apart. However the Park District in Rolling Meadows, a suburb to the northwest of the city, offered space and on December 3, 1993, Fosser opened a charming 65 seat basement theater in the building.[17] Above the proscenium is the slogan "Not only

Bill Fosser with
Shayne (*left*) and
Justin Snyder (*right*).

for Amusement" – in tribute to the Kungsholm Miniature Grand Opera. At long last Opera in Focus had found a permanent home.

William Fosser's lung cancer returned and part of his right lung was removed. In 2005 the Puppeteers of America honoured him with their President's Award in recognition to his "contribution to the Art of Puppetry." His health continued to decline and he died on February 19, 2006.

Today Justin and Shayne Snyder maintain the Opera in Focus legacy. The brothers had been assistants at the theatre and were carefully mentored by Fosser for some years. Fosser's instructions were if Opera in Focus ever closed down, all the puppets were to be destroyed because he didn't want them to suffer the same ignoble fate of the Kungsholm puppets. Under the guidance of the Snyder brothers, the company continues twice weekly performances (4:00 pm on Wednesdays and 1:30 pm on Saturdays) and new scenes are added to the repertoire each season.

Opera in Focus has recently celebrated its 61st birthday and 25th year at the Park District in Rolling Meadows. Of the three miniature opera companies, it has the longest record of introducing grand opera to audiences who might never experience "the combination of spectacle, lighting, singing, costumes, color, motion, and grandeur"[18] of grand opera.

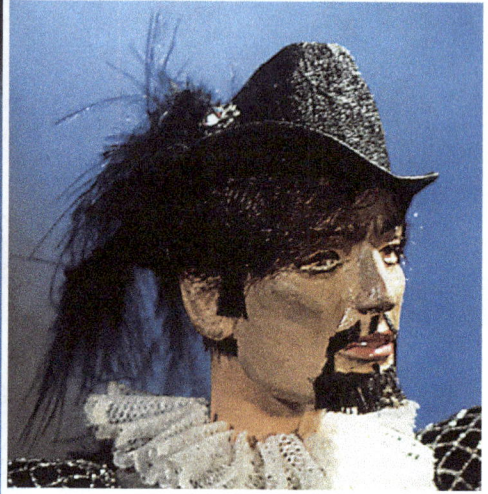

Count di Luna

"Il Trovatore"

Sculpted by Bill Fosser
Costume by Paul Guerra

Magda

"La Rondine"

Sculpted by Bill Fosser
Costume by
Judy Thomson

"Faust"

Lakmé

"Lakmé"

Sculpted by Bill Fosser
Costume by Paul Guerra

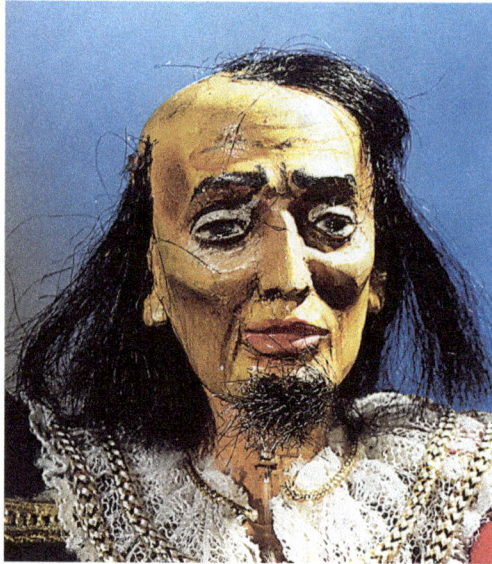

Rigoletto

"Rigoletto"

Sculpted by Bill Fosser
Costume by Paul Guerra

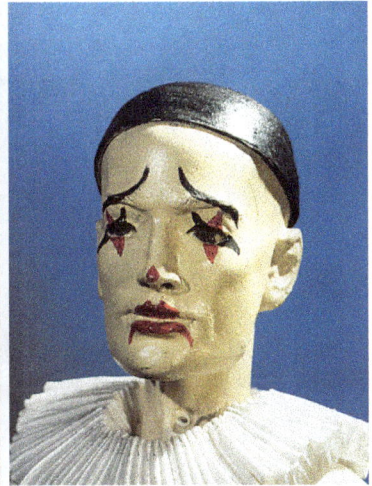

Canio

"Pagliacci"

Sculpted by Bill Fosser
Costume by Paul Guerra

"Lakmé"

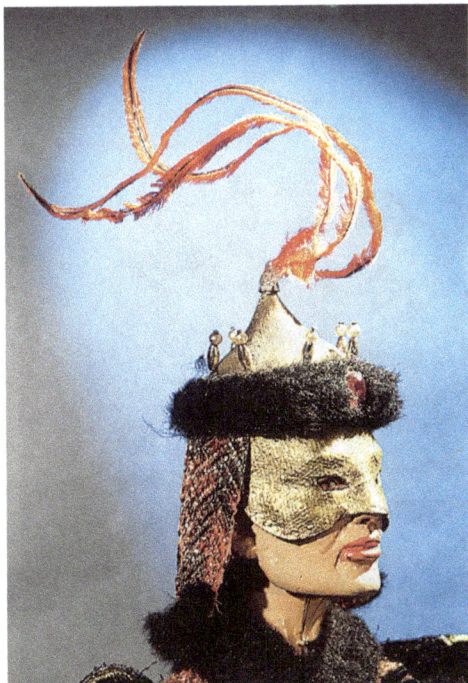

Calaf

"Turandot"

Sculpted by Bill Fosser
Costume by Paul Guerra

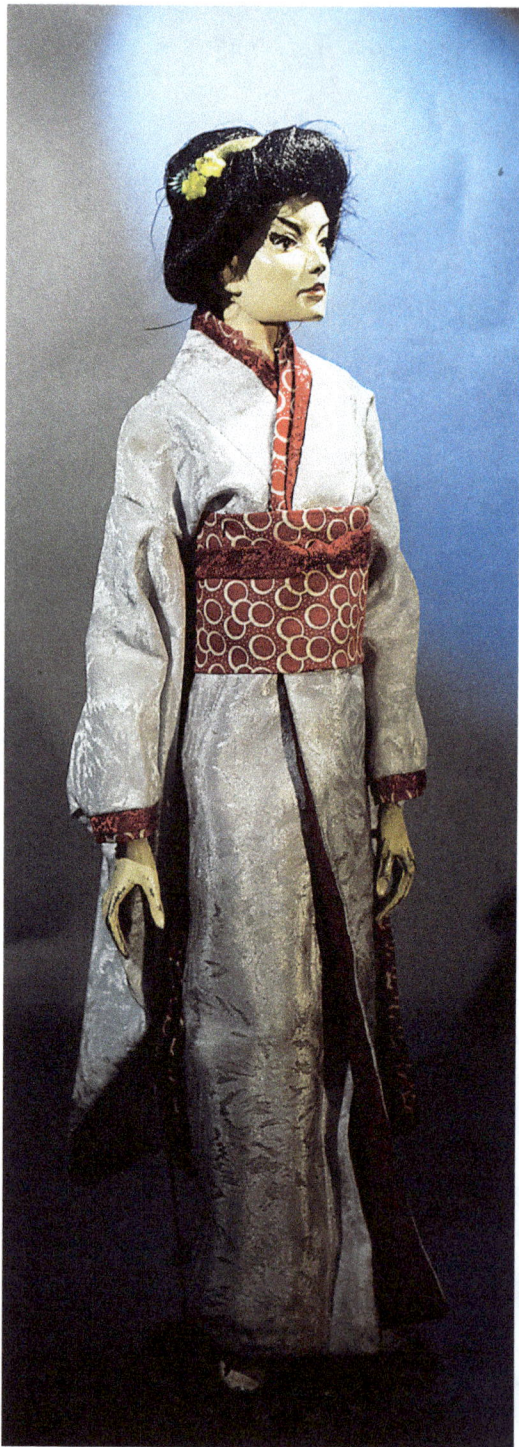

Suzuki

"Madame Butterfly"

Sculpted by Bill Fosser
Costume by Paul Guerra

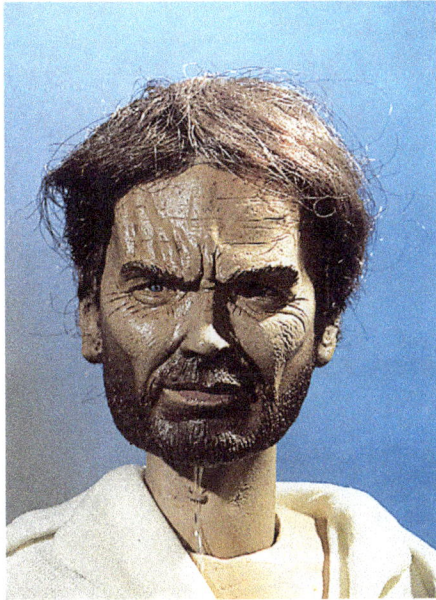

Mario Cavaradossi

"Tosca"

Sculpted by Shayne Snyder
Costume by Paul Guerra

Lohengrin

"Lohengrin"

Sculpted by Bill Fosser
Costume by Paul Guerra

Dorothy Gale

"Wizard of Oz"

Sculpted by Shayne Snyder
Costume by Judy Thomson

Amneris

"Aida"

Sculpted by Bill Fosser
Costume by Paul Guerra

Diva

(Used for Encores and Demonstrations)

Sculpted by Bill Fosser
Costume by Paul Guerra

Mephistophles

"Faust"

Sculpted by Bill Fosser
Costume by Paul Guerra

Dancing Girls

"Opera Stars on Broadway"

Sculpted by Bill Fosser
Costume by Paul Guerra

This Page: *"Boris Godunov"*

Opposite Page: Olympia
"Tales of Hoffman"

Sculpted by Shayne Snyder
Costume by
Paul Guerra

[1] September 5, 1928 – February 19, 2006. www.ancestry.com

[2] Hanna, Janan, "The Phantom Hands of the Opera", *Chicago Tribune*, December 11, 1992. n.p.

[3] Putz, Marilyn & Fred, "William B. Fosser's Puppet Productions Opera in Focus" *Puppetry Journal*, Vol. 49, Issue 4, p. 8.

[4] Ibid.

[5] www.usinflationcalculator.com

[6] Ibid.

[7] Lavin, Cheryl, "Bill Fosser's Small but Grand Opera", *Chicago Tribune Magazine*, reprinted *Puppetry Journal*, Vol. 30, Issue 6, p. 23.

[8] www.usinflationcalculator.com

[9] Swanton, Mary, "Puppet Love: Bill Fosser's Quest to Keep Miniature Opera Alive." *City Talk*, June 7-20, 2002, p.10.

[10] Putz, Marilyn & Fred, "William B. Fosser's Puppet Productions Opera in Focus" *Puppetry Journal*, Vol. 49, Issue 4, p. 8

[11] Ibid.

[12] Putz, Marilyn & Fred, "William B. Fosser's Puppet Productions Opera in Focus" *Puppetry Journal*, Vol. 49, Issue 4, p. 8

[13] Gary Jones, e-mail to author dated December 26, 2018.

[14] Putz, Fred, "In Memoriam: William B. Fosser", *Puppetry Journal*, 57-3-9.

15 Ibid.

[16] Putz, Marilyn & Fred, "William B. Fosser's Puppet Productions Opera in Focus" *Puppetry Journal* Vol. 49, Issue 4, p. 8

[17] Ibid.

[18] *Chicago Guide*, n.d., n.p.

Appendix 1 - **The Wolff Rod Puppet**

THE WOLFF ROD PUPPET is different from traditional rod puppets. Instead of being held over the puppeteer's head, it stands on the stage floor and is operated by wires and strings extending down through slots in the floor to the puppeteer beneath.

Having agreed to perform at the 1939 New York World's Fair, Ernest realized the six-inch German dolls he had been using would be too small for the venue. With so many puppets to be created in the short time before the World's Fair, a standardized figure had to be devised. So while Ernest built a larger stage, scenery, and props, Mme. Wolff and Fred Stauffer, a family friend, developed a 13" tall puppet with limited head and arm movements. At that time, most marionettes and rod puppets had wooden bodies but the torso of the Wolff rod puppet is a cage-like construction of wire. It obviously was inspired by the dressmaker's wire-form dress dummy which Mrs. Wolff would have known. A lampshade frame manufacturer was commissioned to mass produce the basic puppet bodies.[1]

The head, arms, and lower legs were carved in wood. Ernest sculpted a male and a female head then a commercial wood carving company produced 48 heads at a time from the models. The arms and feet were similarly mass produced.[2]

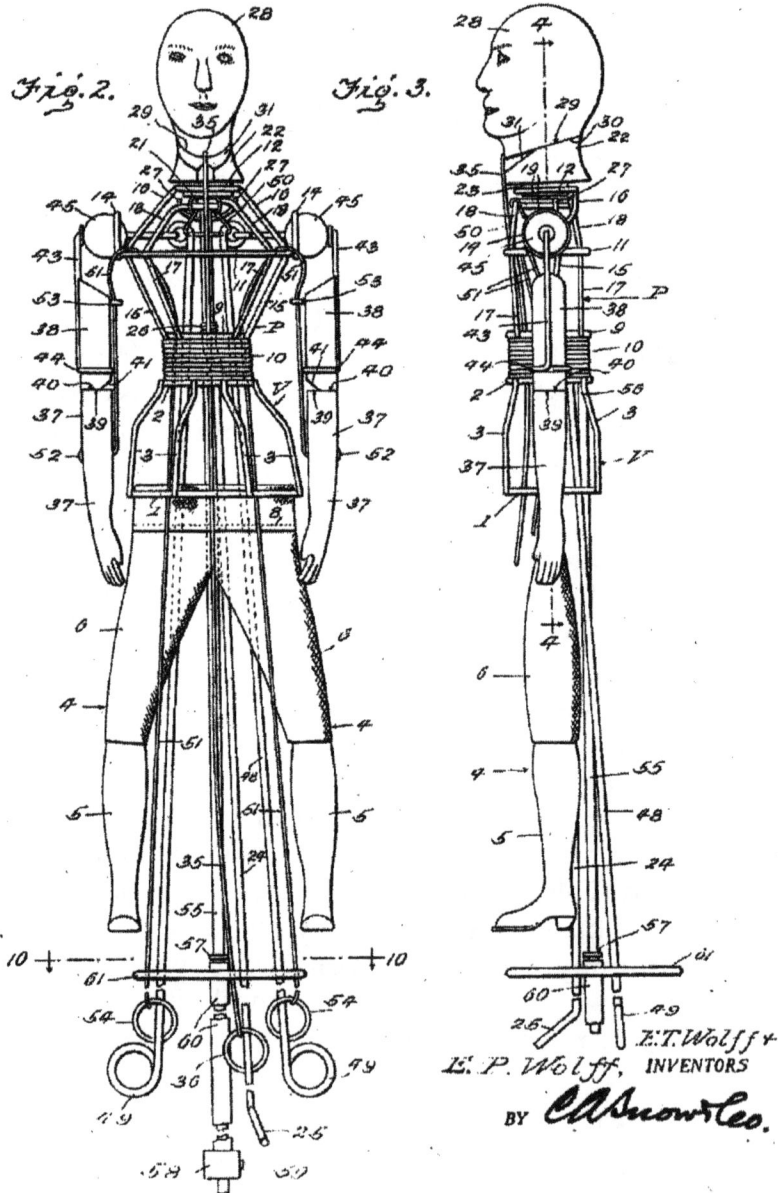

Fig. 2.   Fig. 3.

E.T.Wolff +

E. P. Wolff, INVENTORS

BY C.A.Snow & Co.

- 130 -

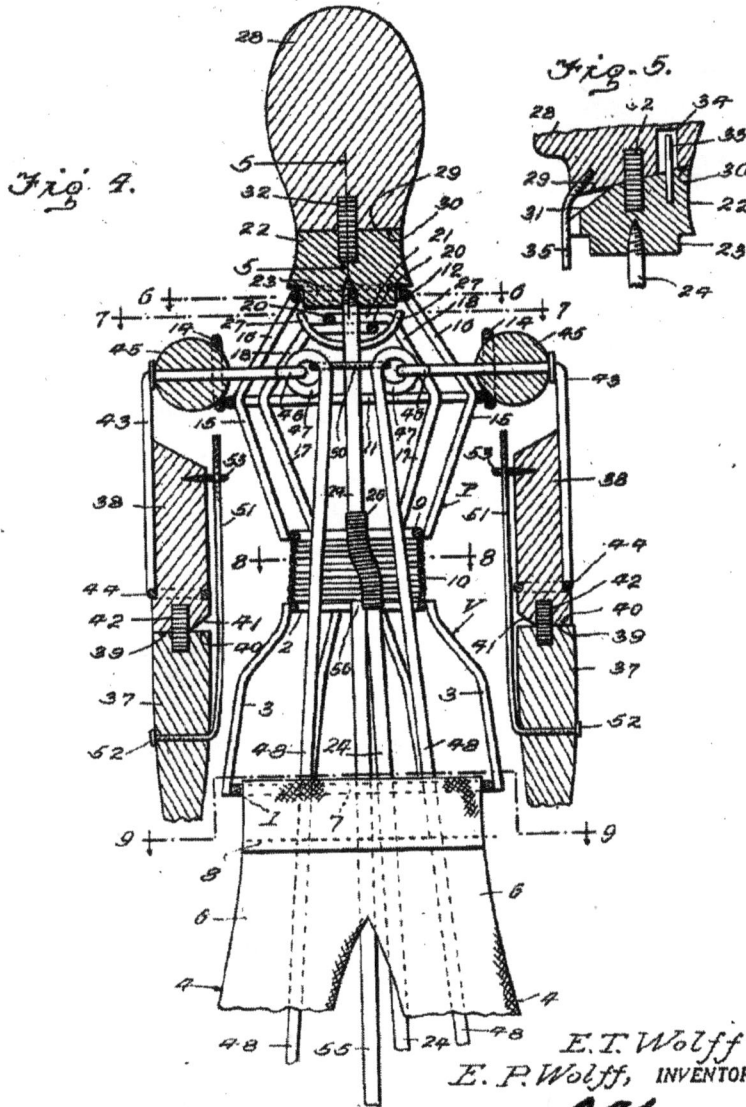

Fig. 4.

Fig. 5.

E. T. Wolff +
E. P. Wolff, INVENTORS

BY

Like the German dolls, characters were individualized with painted makeup, wigs, body padding, and costumes.

The new puppets were supported by a stiff metal wire which projected down through a circular metal plate just below the puppet's feet then continued through the slotted stage floor to a metal cylinder which served as a handle as well as a counterweight to maintain the puppet's upright stance if the puppeteer's grip was released. There were six controls on the puppet. In addition to the support wire, a second stiff wire, attached to the neck, enabled the head to be turned and a string attached under the chin made the puppet look down. Rather than a mechanical joint, a small spring connected the head to the neck. This kept the puppet's head upright unless the string was deliberately pulled to make the head bow.

A stiff wire was linked to each shoulder joint so the arms could be lifted out sideways from the body and moved to some degree in other directions. Each arm had a string attached to the wooden lower arm. It ran in front of the elbow to the bicep of the wooden upper arm, then to the shoulder joint and down through the body to the handle at the very bottom. When the string was pulled, the arm would bend at the elbow.

Instead of a tongue-and-groove joint at the elbow, the two wooden arm pieces are joined by a small spring like the head-neck joint. This ensured the arm remained straight unless the string was pulled. However the spring added resistance so the string had to be pulled with some force before the elbow would begin to bend.

The three wires and three strings passed through holes in the metal disk under the puppet's feet then to the handle below the stage floor. Each string was tied to 1-inch metal ring – the head string to the ring encircling the head turning

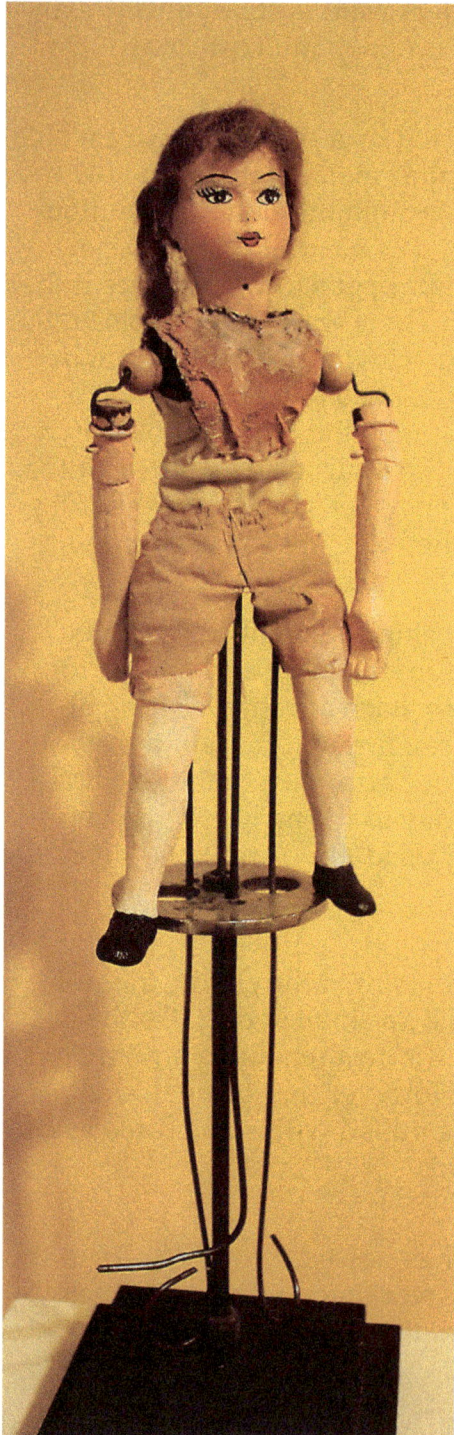

rod, the arms strings to the corresponding rings around each shoulder control.

To move about the stage, the figure was pushed along the slots in the floor.

The original puppets had wooden lower legs hanging from cloth tube upper legs. Later figures had wooden legs with a tongue-and-grove knee joint. The legs were rarely animated by the puppeteers.[3]

Although limited, these movements were sufficient for the rather static actions of an opera performance.[4]

Mme. Wolff researched costumes from the New York Metropolitan, the Scala Opera in Milan, and the Paris Opera House, then created miniature copies. With her couturiere training, she had an awareness of the fabrics and tended to choose thinner and softer materials which draped effectively and moved with the puppets.

The costumes of the Kungsholm puppets, and especially the men's clothing, tend to be made of thicker, less flexible fabrics. The result is stiff, doll-like clothing rather than miniature copies of actual stage costumes. In the thirty year existence off the Kungsholm, costumes were made by a number of people who may not have understood the importance of the fabric's scale and flexibility to the puppet's ability to move. Also some of the existing costumes may have been fashioned when the puppets were restored for the permanent exhibit at the Museum of Science and Industry. The restorers may not have understood the same concept.

Most of the wigs of both the Wolff and Kungsholm companies were fashioned from theatrical crepe hair – a stiff, crinkly, plant-based fibre which is difficult to control on such small figures. Some puppets have wigs of embroidery floss – a material with little body so these wigs tend to quickly flatten and lose shape. Neither material has withstood the improper storage the puppets experienced.

Because the base plate was firmly attached to the supporting rod, sitting or kneeling required the puppet to be positioned at one of the circular openings scattered around the stage floor. The puppeteer then lowered the main rod to maneuver the base plate through the opening. A slot in the chair seat accommodated the rods and strings.

[1] Chamberlain, Charles, "Chicago's famed Kungsholm Puppets perform once more." *Alton Telegraph*, May 14, 1982, p. A-2

[2] Ibid.

[3] Email to author from Gary Jones, January 9, 2019.

[4] U.S. Patent application No. 2,327,234. Filed November 22, 1942.

Appendix 2 - **The Fosser Rod Puppet**

THE ROD PUPPET CREATED by William Fosser is a larger and more refined figure than the Wolff version. Instead of the wire basket body, Fosser's puppet torso and hips are cast in resin, as are the arms and legs. The elbows and knees are well crafted tongue-and-groove joints and the waist joint is a spring or a rubber tube holding the torso upright unless the manipulator makes the puppet bend. The hands and feet are lead castings and the head is individually sculpted rather than mass produced.

The legs can be raised to simulate the puppet taking steps and the arms are controlled by spring-wire rods attached to the palms of the hands. These rods enable broader and more expressive arm movements than the Wolff puppet.

Another difference is the base plate beneath the puppet's feet. The Fosser puppet has a cast metal disc which is larger than the Wolff base. Rather than standing atop the stage floor, the plate slides in grooves in the sides of the floor slots. This ensures the puppet remains upright without need of a counter-weight at the bottom of the main support rod. The base plate is not permanently attached to the main support rod. Turning the rod slightly will unlock it, then the rod can be lowered to make the puppet sit or kneel while the base plate remains secure in the grooves along the sides of the stage floor slot.

July 9, 1968 W. B. FOSSER **3,391,485**

NECK AND HEAD JOINT FOR A PUPPET

Original Filed Oct. 23, 1961 6 Sheets-Sheet 3

FIG. 5A

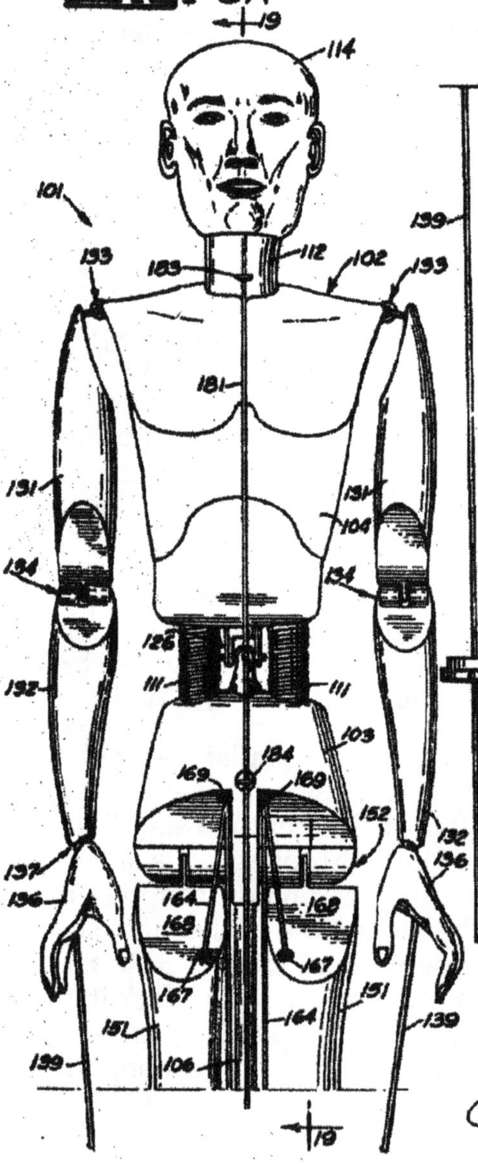

FIG. 5B

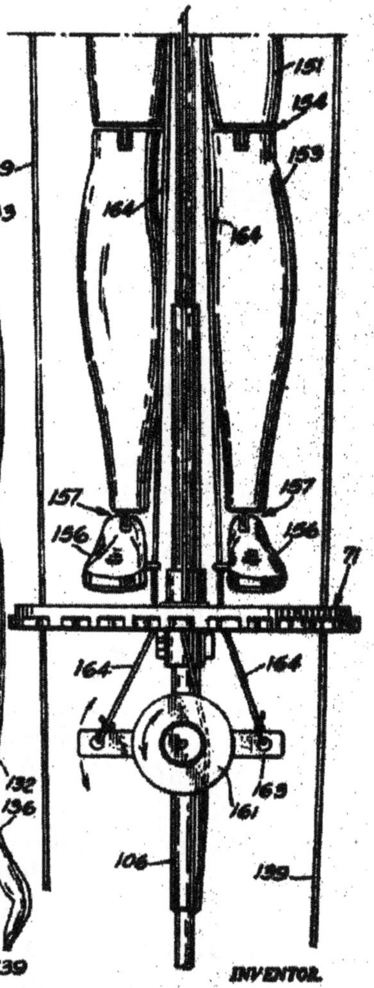

INVENTOR.
WILLIAM B. FOSSER
BY Charles B. Cannon
His Atty.

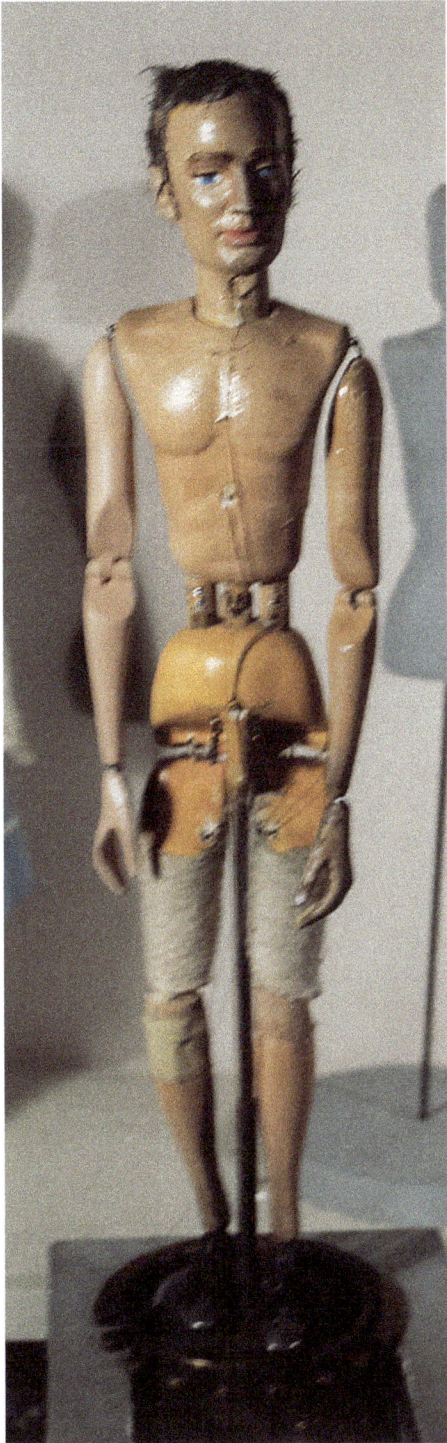

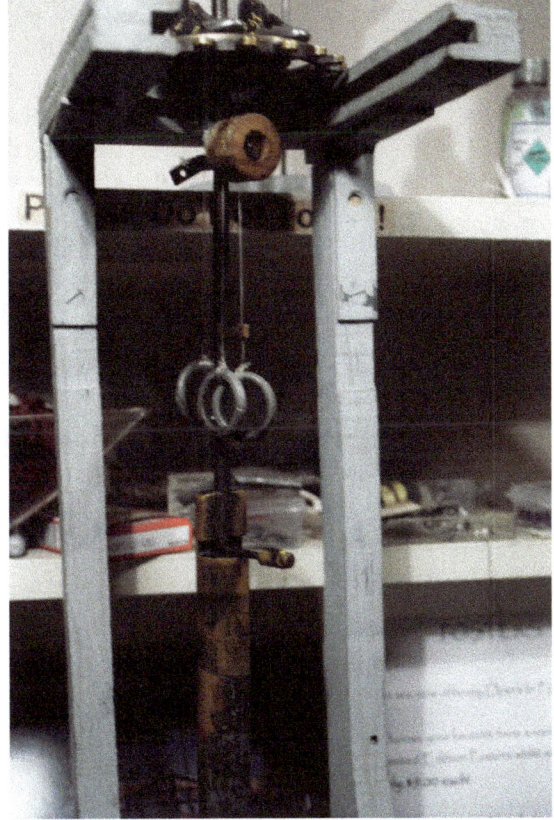

The movement of Fosser puppet head is nearly identical to the Wolff puppet - a rod turns the neck and a string to the chin makes the puppet look down. Another string is attached to the front of the torso to make the puppet bow and a third string is attached to the torso spine to bend the puppet slightly backwards.

A large knob on the control handle operates the puppet's legs. Rotating it back and forth alternately lifts the legs. Each leg string is attached in front of the hip joint and after passing through a tiny pulley in the pelvis, goes down to the appropriate side of the control knob. On the way the string passes through a loop at the puppet's corresponding instep. This guides the foot in a straight up and down movement and prevents it from flipping forward. However it also makes the puppet look as if it is climbing stairs or stepping in place. Rotating the main handle slightly from side to side with each step helps disguise the odd walk.

A thin, straight spring wire is attached to the palm of each hand. This allows a much wider range of expressive movement than the Wolff arm mechanism.

Paul Guerra,[1] who created many of the Fosser costumes, was a teenager when he met Fosser, then the director of the Kungsholm opera. Over the years the two created a number of productions and Guerra's costumes are outstanding. The fabrics are perfectly suited to the scale of the puppet resulting in elegant and detailed costumes which move with the puppet rather than impede its actions.

---

[1] June 30, 1944 - August 8, 2007. *Chicago Tribune*, August 18, 2007, n.p.

Appendix 3 - Sample Repertories

N ITS EARLY YEARS, the Kungsholm Miniature Grand Opera changed the production each day - as is the practice of regular opera companies. This was possible because the theatre staff included several stage hands as well as the puppeteers, a sound and a lighting technician, plus the ushers in the auditorium. The photo below was taken during that period shows the week's roster of six different productions which changed daily.

However by the 1960's, the staff had been reduced to five or six puppeteers, a lighting/sound technician in the control room, and a single greeter/usher in the auditorium. With the limited staff, production changes occurred only bi-weekly.

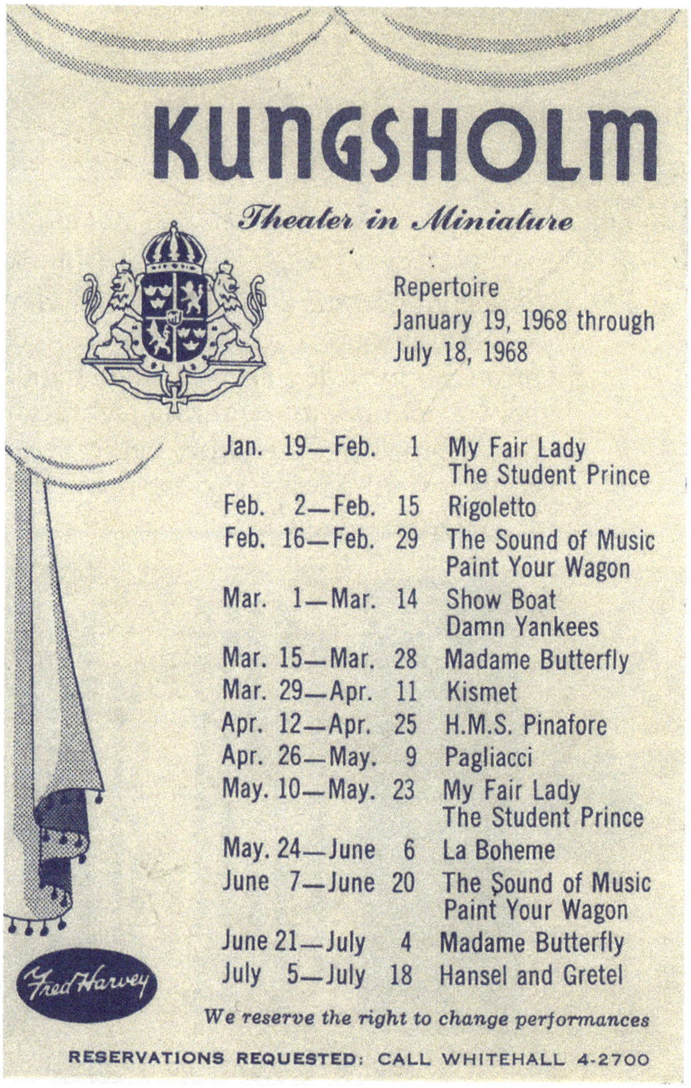

KUNGSHOLM

Theater in Miniature

Repertoire
January 19, 1968 through
July 18, 1968

Jan. 19—Feb. 1	My Fair Lady
	The Student Prince
Feb. 2—Feb. 15	Rigoletto
Feb. 16—Feb. 29	The Sound of Music
	Paint Your Wagon
Mar. 1—Mar. 14	Show Boat
	Damn Yankees
Mar. 15—Mar. 28	Madame Butterfly
Mar. 29—Apr. 11	Kismet
Apr. 12—Apr. 25	H.M.S. Pinafore
Apr. 26—May. 9	Pagliacci
May. 10—May. 23	My Fair Lady
	The Student Prince
May. 24—June 6	La Boheme
June 7—June 20	The Sound of Music
	Paint Your Wagon
June 21—July 4	Madame Butterfly
July 5—July 18	Hansel and Gretel

Fred Harvey

We reserve the right to change performances

RESERVATIONS REQUESTED: CALL WHITEHALL 4-2700

www.ingramcontent.com/pod-product-compliance
Lightning Source LLC
Chambersburg PA
CBHW062012090426

42811CB00005B/828